The Keys To Grapeness

Growing a Spirit-led Life

GIL STIEGLITZ

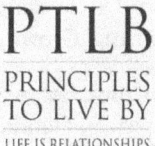

PTLB
PRINCIPLES
TO LIVE BY
LIFE IS RELATIONSHIPS

A Principles To Live By Publication
April 2017

The Keys to Grapeness: Growing a Spirit-led Life
Copyright © 2017 by Gil Stieglitz

Published by Principles to Live By, P.O. Box 214, Roseville CA 95661. For more information about this book and the author, visit www.ptlb.com.

Cover Design by John Chase
Copyedited by Jennifer Edwards @ jedwardsediting.net
Book Design by Kelly Stuber

All Rights reserved. No part of this publication may be reproduced, stored in a retrieval system, or transmitted in any way by an means-electronic, mechanical, photocopy, recording, or otherwise-without the prior permission of the copyright holder, except as provided by USA copyright law.

When reproducing text from this book, include the following credit line: "*The Keys to Grapeness: Growing a Spirit-led Life*" by Gil Stieglitz, published by Principles To Live By Publishing. Used by permission."

ISBN: 978-0-9968855-2-2

RELIGION/Christian Life/Relationships
RELIGION/Christian Ministry/Discipleship
RELIGION/Christian Life/Spiritual Growth

All Scripture verses are from the New American Standard Bible unless otherwise indicated. New American Standard Bible: 1995 update. 1995 La Habra, CA: The Lockman Foundation.

Printed in the United States of America

Contents

A Note to the Reader 5

Introduction 7

How Success Is Defined Matters 17

Relationships Matter More! 29

And the Greatest of These Is Love 37

Joy-Producing Positivity 45

Bringing Harmony, Order, and Calm—Peace 51

Giving Room and Time for Change—Patience 63

The Pleasant Helpfulness of Kindness 71

Doing More Than They Truly Deserve—Goodness 77

Meekness Is Not Weakness 87

Stay the Course with Faithfulness 93

Moderate Your Desires with Self-Control 99

Practice Standing in Each Garden 107

Conclusion: A Look at Proverbs 11:30 115

About Gil Stieglitz 119

More from Principles To Live By 121

A Note to the Reader

Now you can easily access Dr. Gil's video course! Scan the QR codes placed throughout the book with your electronic device. Dr. Gil personally explains the concepts further and encourages you throughout the process. All you need is a QR Code scanning app, which can be downloaded for free on iTunes or Google Play. Just scan the code and it will take you directly to the video. You can also access the videos by typing the address, which is listed next to the QR code, into your web browser. We hope you enjoy this interactive element. Please feel free to provide us any feedback by emailing info@ptlb.com.

— Principles To Live By Publishing

www.ptlb.com

Sample URL and QR code

Introduction

One of the incredible perks of becoming a Christian is receiving the Holy Spirit as our guide for life. God wants to do in us and through us what we cannot do ourselves—to partner with us to develop qualities, actions, reactions, and attitudes that will develop a wonderful life. If we don't partner with Him, then we are left with the best we can do on our own. And because we are human, many of the essential qualities for a delightful and significant life will be missing. When we partner with the Holy Spirit, He will guide us by telling us what to say, what to do, when to do it, along with the ability to say and do those things that are not in us by nature. I know this power to be real and true.

www.ptlb.com/
grapeness-intro

Before I was nineteen years old, I could not say the words "I love you" to anyone. I simply could not say them. Only when I was taught how to let the Holy Spirit prompt me to love others and express my love in various ways was I able to say those words and mean them—and not just in a romantic setting! Recently, I have found the Holy Spirit wants to partner with me to develop a whole new level of joy in my life. It's thrilling! Recently, I was in a situation where there was a lot of difficulty and disorder. I was focused on the problems and experienced much angst and anxiety. The Lord started whispering to me, "notice the good," "focus on the good in people," "find the things that are delightful," "enjoy the good times no matter how brief." As I have agreed with these whispers, my whole demeanor has changed, and my ability to cope with a very difficult situation has completely transformed. Some people who know me personally and know about the situation have remarked about the wonder of it all! It is the Holy Spirit and my partnership with Him. If it were up to me alone, I would be mad, irritable, and defiant without Him. I want you to experience this same sense of joy and peace.

This book is meant to help you grow a Spirit-led life, one where you can hear the whispers of God as He speaks into your life. It begins by prayerfully reading through the fruit of the Spirit in Galatians 5:22-23.

> *"But the fruit of the Spirit is love, joy, peace, forbearance, kindness, goodness, faithfulness, gentleness and self-control. Against such things there is no law."*

Introduction

My hope is that this will be a simple, instructive guide to a spiritual exercise I recommend doing every day. It involves prayerful, slow recitation of the fruit of the Spirit, accompanied by attentiveness to the Spirit of Christ's whispers, which He gives back to you about the fruit He wants to grow through you. Personally, I choose to do this in the morning, however some prefer to do this at night before bed. Lunch time or midday is good too—it's really whatever works best for you. The key is to have some quiet, concentrated time to pray and listen for God's prompting through His Spirit.

The process entails going over the basic aspects of the fruit of the Spirit one-by-one to get a sense of what God wants you to do, say, or focus on at that moment or within the next few hours or day. He may be trying to get you to change the way you behave or your attitude regarding one of your relationships, or to do something in a particular situation or activity. The wonder of the Holy Spirit is that He knows what you need to add to your life to maximize your potential. Oh if we would only listen to what He is saying! The early church believers took this idea of partnering with the Holy Spirit much more serious than we do today. They expected God to whisper to them and direct them to create a different life than they could create on their own. At that time, new Christians needed to get used to the promptings and whispers of the Holy Spirit. They were given the various lists (see Gal 5:22,23; 1 Pet 1:5-10; Matt 5:3-12) of what the Holy Spirit would say to them so they could discern which promptings were coming from the Holy Spirit and which were coming from the devil, themselves, or the world.

As I was trained in this aspect of the Christian life, I was told, "If you sense a prompting to do something loving, joyful, peaceful, or any other of the fruit of the Spirit, then do it. That is the Holy Spirit." As you grow in your knowledge of the Lord Jesus Christ and the Holy Spirit, you will get better and better at discerning what God is saying to you. We often make it so complicated. God comes to live within us when we become Christians and He wants to guide us to a much better life than we could ever have without Him. Yes, I know that we have to be on alert for false promptings of the devil, the world, and the flesh, but we often scare people so much about the false promptings that we make them afraid to follow the positive promptings of the Holy Spirit! Some people get really wrapped up in the idea that communicating with God involves some higher form of spirituality, but it doesn't. It really is quite simple.

My life is completely different than it would have ever become without the guidance of the Holy Spirit. The more I follow the whispers of the Holy Spirit—to love others when I want to hold back, to be patient with people when I would write them off, to exercise self-control instead of indulgence, to be kind when I would be sarcastic—the more my life changes. I make friends with people I would have pushed past. I receive job offers that would never have come. I learn new things where I would have stayed ignorant. I develop closeness with people where I would have been way too protective. I can say without reservation that my marriage is completely different for the better; my career is more significant; my finances are

Introduction

much better; my friendships are wonderfully diverse and rich; my church experiences and involvements are tremendously full and more moving. The narrow little world I would have inhabited without the guidance of the Holy Spirit cannot be compared with the life the Holy Spirit has given me.

It all starts with a little exercise of listening to the Holy Spirit in a regular and systematic way. Prayerfully and slowly repeat the fruit of the Spirit (Love, Joy, Peace, Patience, Kindness, Goodness, Gentleness, Faithfulness, and Self-Control) listening for the urging of the Holy Spirit on one of them towards one of your relationships. If we take the time to tune in to the Holy Spirit, it will be surprising what He will say and what will begin to happen as you move forward at His impulse. It is sometimes counterintuitive, but when you understand that God is for love, joy, peace, and so forth, it will make perfect sense.

Sometimes I need to develop a new level of one of these fruits—more love, more patience, more goodness, and so on—so He puts a picture of me doing something that I am not inclined to do, like the dishes, vacuuming, apologizing, calling someone, taking a job I don't want, reading a book or article, reaching out to someone... Sometimes He has desires for me to reach for a whole new level in one of my relationships—I need to step up my game and let more of Him flow through me to people in my life. Sometimes God alerts me to *the who* I am to direct one of these qualities toward later that day. The goal here is to dialogue with the Holy Spirit, so you can be ready to strengthen your relationships by practicing and using these fruits of the Spirit.

Yes, sometimes I argue with the Holy Spirit about some of the things He seems to be prompting me to do, just as Ananias argued with the Lord in Acts 9: 10-16, "Lord, you couldn't want me to say that to that person!" Just the other day, I said some things during a time of banter and fun that the Lord wanted me to apologize for because they could be construed as insensitive and offensive. The Lord and I went back and forth for over an hour before I realized that He was right—I apologized to the person. It was well received, and it helped to deepen my friendship with this person.

In practice, I just repeat each of the fruits slowly and prayerfully letting God lead me to the relationship or the person that this particular "fruit" applies to. Sometimes it is clear that God wants me to focus on one of the qualities in all my relationships. Just the other evening, my wife was talking to me about something that was very important to her. To her, though, it seemed like I wasn't listening. I really was listening, so I wanted to ramp up and defend myself while she was telling me her point of view! The Lord just kept whispering, "hold back," "don't power up," "listen to what she is saying." My natural self wanted to defend my actions and prove to her I was listening, but the only way to do that was to listen to her tell me that she thought I wasn't listening. The Holy Spirit kept me from making a mess of the evening. He helped me to "say" that I was listening by really listening to her tell me that she thought I wasn't listening to her!

Every so often, God makes it very clear to me that I have major work to do in one of these qualities (or fruits) or in one of my relationships. He will put me in a situation where I really feel anger, hatred, depression, fear, bitterness, superiority, or envy toward a person. This is how He often points out that we have major work to do. He begins to suggest that I do something loving, joyful, or peaceful directed at this person or in the situation. In this way, God the Holy Spirit seeks to improve another aspect of my life. I have to make the decision whether I am going to partner with Him in this arena or with this person. If I decide to ignore His promptings, then the relationship or situation stays dysfunctional or dead. If I let Him know that I am willing to let Him grow His fruit in this area or relationship, then the partnership is on. I know that my life is about to take a leap forward. Yes, it may be painful, because I will have to be willing to do things that don't come naturally for me, but in truth, they are really better for my spiritual, emotional, mental, and physical wellbeing.

There are times when I grieve the Holy Spirit, because I am unwilling to do what He clearly suggests. This does not end our relationship, though, which is important to understand. God does not deny us just because we have been unfaithful. He stays faithful always (2 Tim 2:13). The Lord Jesus died to pay for our sins and wants us to re-engage with Him through confession and humble obedience. Just start listening again. Just start obeying. Let Him know that you messed up and didn't listen. Accept His forgiveness and start again. What does He want you to know? Does He still want you to do the same thing as before, or is that assignment in the past? God is not here to condemn us but to partner with us, so we can accomplish the life He has planned for us (Eph 2:10).

I like to think of the Christian life like a tightrope walk. God wants us to walk across the tightrope and get to the other side. It is a narrow path, and there is not much room for error. But He has put the safety net of the life, death, and resurrection of Jesus Christ underneath us. When we fall and fail to make the kind of progress that He has planned for us, we fall off into the loving arms of the Lord Jesus, who loved us and gave Himself up for us. We are to confess our sins and climb back up the pole and start making progress on the tightrope with the guidance of the Holy Spirit. God is not here to condemn us (Rom 8:1); He is here to help us make progress in our life. He wants us to succeed and produce in our life what is clearly beyond us, so that people will see Him in us (Col 1:27; Rom 8:14).

You may struggle with this process at first; I did too. But if, as you read this list slowly and prayerfully, one of qualities really sticks out, or you react to it in some way, like your heart rate bumps up or your eyes focus intensely, pay attention! That is where God wants to work. Be mindful if a particular person comes to mind when you read one of these definitions. Start taking with God about that person and the quality that God connected to him or her.

If He is whispering...

... Love, that means you are to be sensitive to the Holy Spirit in how He wants you to meet someone's needs, pursue their soul, or please them.

Introduction

... Joy, that means you are to be alert when God the Holy Spirit whispers, "notice the good, the encouraging, and the positive in the other person, in this relationship, in this situation..."

... Peace, that means you are to listen to the Holy Spirit when He urges you to be in harmony with someone or to bring order to a relationship or to keep calm.

... Patience, that means you are to listen to the Holy Spirit when He says, "give more time, give the person more room, and give space to grow and fail."

... Kindness, that means you are to be alert to the Holy Spirit when He emphasizes how you help people in a pleasant way.

... Goodness, that means that you are to be sensitive to God's whispers about truly benefiting the other person(s) in a way they don't necessarily deserve—spiritually, mentally, emotionally, financially, relationally, or physically.

... Meekness, that means you are to look to the Holy Spirit immediately when you are angry, knowing you may have embraced unrealistic expectations. Then listen for His wise adaptions and thoughtful requests.

... Faithfulness, that means you are to obey the whispers of the Holy Spirit to "keep loving and stay connected to this person."

... Self-control, that means you are to adapt to the Lord's voice when He says, "moderate your desires for the sake of the relationship."

I hope this book is useful to you as you learn to let the Holy Spirit lead you to a great life of success and joy.

1.
How Success Is Defined Matters

Jesus replied: "'Love the Lord your God with all your heart and with all your soul and with all your mind.' This is the first and greatest commandment. And the second is like it: 'Love your neighbor as yourself.'" (Matt 22:37-39)

I believe that many people have the wrong definition of success—that is, one based upon the world's measurements: piles of money, pleasure, fame, power, beauty, possessions, and the like. I want to suggest that Jesus gave us a very different

www.ptlb.com/
grapeness-ch1

definition of what a successful life looks like. In Matthew 22:37-39, he said the two greatest commandments are to love God with all our heart, soul, mind, and strength, and to love our neighbor as ourselves. In two short sentences, Jesus tells us the secret to a successful life—success is filling our lives with strong, loving relationships. It is not how many toys or material things you end up with before you die, but rather who will miss you when you're long gone.

You might be curious to know that scientists have actually done studies of the places where people live the longest and seem to have the most joy in their lives. These are called "blue zones." In every one of these places around the globe, people put the focus of their energies on relationships, not possessions. According to Dan Beuttner, author of *The Blue Zones: 9 Lessons for Living Longer From the People Who've Lived the Longest*[1], "The recipe for longevity is deeply intertwined with community, lifestyle, and spirituality." Yes. They do eat healthy diets, but their happiness is based on the strength and depth of relationships. Relationships are very important to them and their lives are more joyful. I agree with this premise.

We All Want a Few Simple Things

Everyone basically wants the same things in life, but we are easily deceived into going after other things instead of pursuing our relationships. If you get down to it, the basic things we want are:

---

1   Buettner, Dan. *The Blue Zones: Lessons for Living Longer From the People Who've Lived the Longest.* Washington, D. C.: National Geographic Society, 2008.

- A deep, interactive connection to God
- To maximize personal potential
- A great marriage to a loving person
- A loving family
- Fruitful and fulfilling career (significant, honorable, and meaningful work)
- Dynamic church that expands and extends our impact
- Safe and attractive community to live in
- Enjoyable and deep friendships
- Abundant and reliable finances
- Peace with our enemies

It is encouraging to think that Jesus and the Holy Spirit want to help us get these things by growing the fruit of the Spirit in each of our relationships (love, joy, peace, patience, kindness, goodness, gentleness, faithfulness, and self-control). God knows that this is the pathway to joy-filled, successful living. We'll learn how to harvest each fruit in the following chapters.

We All Crave Deep Connection

What do we need to do to have great, meaningful relationships? We are so often wrong about this area. We think that if we find people who have the same interests we do, we'll be happy. Or, if we can just find someone who will like us, we will be okay. But we don't know how to go deeper than the surface with them. In so many cases, we have to pay people to listen to us, because we don't know how to have great give-and-take relationships.

In an age of cell phones, tweets, emails, texts, and Facebook posts, we have never been so lonely. People crave connection but don't do the things to bring that about. So how do we move past the surface and move into depth with other people? Let me help you understand how to connect with people and then explain how these tools can be used to change your life. The following actions are the basics of how to go deeper with others. This is truly the list of the actions that you and I must take to make a relationship work and go deeper. Look at them and then follow the Holy Spirit in doing them.

- Sacrifice to meet their needs (love)

- Continue to pursue them (love)

- Please them (love)

- Have positive focus (joy)

- Harmony, calm, and bringing order (peace)

- Giving time and room for change (patience)

- Attitude of pleasant helpfulness (kindness)

- Adding benefit to their lives (goodness)

- Staying connected to them (faithfulness)

- Setting realistic expectations, exercising impulse control, giving thoughtful requests, and practicing wise adaptation (gentleness)

- Moderation of desires (self-control)

Sounds easy, right? Except that we have three problems with this list. We don't know *how* to do these things, we don't know *who* to do them to, and we don't know *when* to do them. Again, this is why I am going to suggest that we need to partner with the Holy Spirit to teach us, prompt us, and train us in the how, who, and when of relationships.

The above list is really just the fruit of the Spirit (Gal 5:22,23) written in a little bit more of a modern form. It is these actions, words, and attitudes that the Holy Spirit of Christ is trying to push through us. When we allow Him in to do these things through us, our relationships will go to a whole other level. They will go deeper as the other person responds. You will experience more love, joy, peace, patience, and so on, in your life, and it will be thrilling. I can't wait until you experience this!

It Begins with Prayer

Prayer is the mechanism to experience the Spirit's leading. Pray slowly through the above list and let God talk to you as you do. In this way, you will begin to live a supernatural life and experience interactive dialogue with the Holy Spirit—this, then, is the Spirit-led life.

The process might look something like this:

Pray saying, "Lord, are you're asking me to sacrifice to meet someone's needs?" Pause to see if God brings anyone to mind to show love to in this way. If He does, then have a dialogue with God about what this is all about with this person. Work out with God the when, where, and what of His whispers to you. Then move on to the next relational action.

As you move down the list, we look at the second aspect of love, "the need to continue to pursue." Ask God if there is someone you need to "continue to pursue" and pause. Does God want you to continue to pursue anyone that you are about to give up on or have already given up on? Have a discussion with God about whatever He brings up in this area of continuing to pursue. If God doesn't bring something up here, then move on to the next quality.

"Please them" is the next relational action that will deepen a relationship if it is done at the right time in the right way. Ask God, "Is there anyone that I need to go beyond the ordinary and please them in some way?" If God brings someone to mind, then have a discussion about what you could do or who to talk to about what might please that person.

The next relational requirement for a growing meaningful relationship is based on joy—positive focus. It is so easy to have a negative focus, isn't it? We naturally notice what is wrong with our life. It is our nature to focus on the bad, the difficult, the wrong, and the irritating. God wants to supply

His energy in the opposite direction. Ask God if there are good, positive, and encouraging things that you should spend more time focusing on. If He brings some wins and some good stuff to mind, that means the answer is *yes*. I know it is easy to say that these few good things would be so much better if this or that or something else were different, but that sucks the life out of the joy God is trying to show you. *Focus on the good that is there.* Ask God how to focus on the good. Go back and forth with Him about what He wants you to focus on and why there is so little of it.

An often-overlooked series of actions that are necessary for great relationships is harmony, calm and order—peace aspects. Every one of us wants our relationships built around our ideas, our plans, and our authority. But that is not how great relationships work. We need to become harmonious with people who are unlike us. We need to stay calm when what we really want is to explode. We must introduce order to our relationships that is beneficial for all, not just for us. Ask God who it is that He wants you to harmonize with and not lead or ignore. When He brings someone to mind, have a dialogue or even a fight about it—don't just ignore the thought. Ask God, "Who do I need to remain calm with today that I will most likely be tempted to become emotional with in some way?" When He brings someone to mind, dialogue about your lack of calm in the past and why you need to be calm with this person this day. Ask God, "Which relationship cannot continue in the chaos it is presently in?" Ask Him what kind of order He wants you to bring to this relationship. How do the other person and you win in the order you think God wants you to win? If the system, order, or rules you want to bring does not produce a win for everybody, it is probably not from God.

Giving a person time and room for change requires patience. Some relationships need to be longer and paced differently than we may want them to be. Ask God if there is any relationship you are ready to cut off, but God wants you to hang in there. Let Him speak and have a dialogue about that relationship and that person. What changes do you and the other person need to make? What does the relationship need? How long will those changes really take? I know God wants to have these kinds of dialogues with you, because He has said that loving relationships is His number one priority (Matt 22:37-39). This is consistent with what we know about Him.

Would people describe you as kind? Ask God how you can exemplify the idea of kindness that Jesus demonstrated when He was here on earth. Who does God want you to be kinder towards? Ask God what forms of pleasant helpfulness you can perform for this person. Interact with God in your spirit and let Him lead you to an action that comes from Him. Yes, you will have to act and speak in ways that are not "you," but this is where the Holy Spirit produces fruit through your life. People need this and you need this. Let it happen.

It was said about Jesus that He went about doing good. Many of us are just going about. God the Holy Spirit wants to start doing good things through you. Ask God if there are any ways that you can truly benefit the people in your life?

What comes to your mind? It will surely be different from one person to the next. Look at doing these things and dialogue with God about them. Let me say that sometimes we want to do some grand gesture and get the goodness thing over. God is not usually involved in that kind of thing. He usually wants the small, regular, truly beneficial thing, like listening, smiling, or helping in some way (1 Cor 13:1-8).

There are some people who are trying to get away from us, but God whispers that we need to stay connected in some way. Ask God who those people may be. Ask Him how He wants you to keep interacting with this person. I have found that God brings to mind all kinds of ways to keep in touch with a person. There are times when God brings a person to mind, and we may think, "That person!" Listen to the Lord.

Unrealistic expectations and lack of impulse control are two of the acids that eat through relational bonds. God the Holy Spirit wants to guide us and empower us to make thoughtful requests, recalibrate our expectations, and adjust through wise adaptations. He will suggest when to request, when to adapt, and when to examine our expectations. Ask God if you have unrealistic expectations about a particular relationship or person. Listen and let God grow a new level of gentleness in that relationship. I have watched fathers destroy the relationship with their children because of unrealistic expectations. I have watched marriages become business relationships, because a wife will not back off of the unrealistic expectations she has for her husband. If our relationships are going to thrive, we must allow God to grow in and through us this quality of meekness, or gentleness. It would be easier to be meek if other people were perfect, but they are not. Ask God how to be wiser and more thoughtful in a particular relationship that is driving you nuts right now. Realistic expectations, impulse control, thoughtful requests, and wise adaptations are at the center of meekness.

The final essential of relationship building is moderation of desires, or self-control. If any two people are going to get along and connect, then there must be moderation of both of their desires. If one or both people are increasingly selfish, then a growing relationship is impossible. One or both must tone down the selfishness. Ask God the Holy Spirit where and how you need to moderate a desire you have so that the relationship will grow. Expect that God will bring something to your mind. Dialogue with Him about it.

There are all kinds of people who would love to go deeper with us, but it may not always be the people that we would choose to go deeper with. Our day and age constantly ranks people—we all only want to develop relationship with people who will help us in some way or who are valuable to us in some way. God the Holy Spirit often does not follow that advice and He wants us to invest in the people who are willing to invest back in us. Remember, the majority of the people on the planet have rejected God, but He continues to reach out to them. Many people are just too busy and too consumed with their own agenda to connect with God (Luke 14:16-24).

How Success Is Defined Matters

Don't be deceived; learn what it takes to have great relationships and *delight* in them. It is the whole of these relationships that make up a great, successful life.

2.
Relationships Matter More!

As a pastor, I have had the unique privilege of coaching and mentoring lots of different kinds of people, including other pastors, businessmen and women, married couples, entrepreneurs, writers, teenagers, and so forth. Whenever I sit down with one of them, I want them to understand the biblical understanding of success—it's one of the first things I do. Inevitably, life is not going the way they want it to go (that's why they called me!), so I have them look at the various relationships of their life to see if they have put all their time,

www.ptlb.com/
grapeness-ch2

energy, or money into a few relationships at the expense of the other ones. Then I have them memorize the two great commandments of Matthew 22:37-39 and repeat these verses as they go to bed at night for a week. It is always amazing how God speaks to people who pay attention to His word.

> *Jesus replied: "'Love the Lord your God with all your heart and with all your soul and with all your mind.' This is the first and greatest commandment. And the second is like it: 'Love your neighbor as yourself.' (Matt 22:37-39)*

Scripture suggests that we can look at our lives as a set of relational gardens (John 15:1-17; Matt 22:37-39). I have identified ten such "gardens" that, when tended to in the proper way, lead to an abundant, full, and prosperous life. The first major relationship is our relationship with God, then self, spouse (if applicable), children, work, church, money, friends, community, and enemies. If we want to have a healthy, joy-filled life, it is up to each of us to grow the fruit of the Spirit in each of these relational gardens of our lives.

God has really put us in charge of nine gardens. We are to cultivate crops of love in each of the gardens, and we get to enjoy life based on the fruit that we have worked with God to grow in these gardens. Whenever we fail in a relationship, that is where the tenth relational garden comes in to play—enemies. The goal in life should be to have as few enemies as possible.

The first nine relational gardens are:

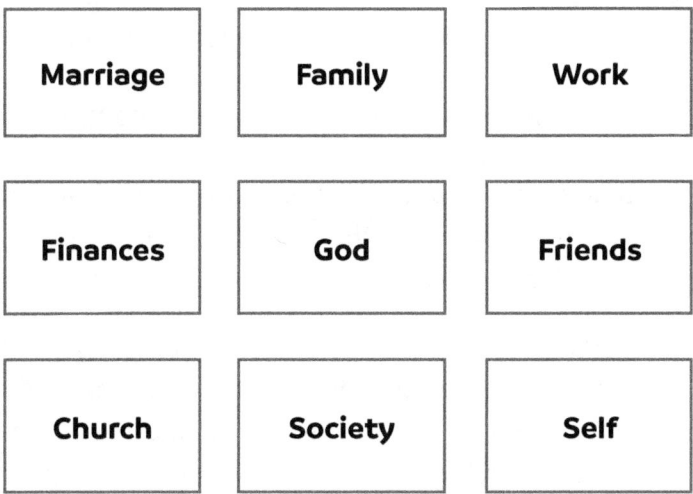

Jesus and the Holy Spirit want to help us grow the fruits of love in each one of these gardens—the fruit of the Spirit in Galatians 5:22,23—love, joy, peace, patience, kindness, goodness, gentleness, faithfulness, and self-control. In other words, the ultimate goal of life is to enjoy a wonderful harvest of love, joy, peace, patience, and so on, from each of the relationships of my life.

Success, then, is measured according to how rich and full each one is. Each relationship can be a tropical rainforest of delights and wonders to enjoy if I will allow Jesus and the Holy Spirit to grow these fruit in that area of my life. In each of my various relationships, I either enjoy a wonderful crop of love and the other qualities, or I move into a desert or a manure pile. You and I are the gardeners of our life. God has given us opportunities, resources, and even direct wisdom, but we must increase the love, joy, peace, and other qualities with the people in our lives, or else our life will be barren of good things.

If I were to mentor you, I would ask you to do three things:

1. Rate each of your gardens on a scale of 1-10 in terms of how much love and the other fruits of the Spirit exist in each relationship.

2. Mentally stand in each of the gardens of your life—picture yourself actually standing there. Ask God what He wants to grow through each one regarding that particular relationship that day: love or joy, peace or patience, kindness or goodness, gentleness, faithfulness, or self-control. He will whisper to you what He knows is needed. Do the gardening work required; in time, there will be a rich, wonderful relationship in that part of your life. There will be a time for harvesting after you have allowed the Holy Spirit to plant, water, grow, and nurture these wonderful qualities into that relational garden.

3. Memorize the Fruit of the Spirit passage, and say it as you fall a sleep for a week. Let God's word drip into your soul and prepare you for the next day's gardening.

"But the fruit of the Spirit is love, joy, peace, patience, kindness, goodness, faithfulness, gentleness, self-control; against such things there is no law."

It is always enlightening for people to stand in each of their relational gardens and really look at what has been growing there—what kind of effort, energy, and resources they have put into that relationship. It is not uncommon for people to realize that they don't know how to grow a relationship of love with their spouse, colleagues, God, children, and so on. This is a wonderful realization, too. Just know that the answers about how to do that are available.

So many people want to walk into the various relationships of their life and just take good things from it without putting in the effort to *grow* good things in that relationship. It takes consistent time, energy, and resources to grow good relationships in each of these gardens. The main relationships take more time, but there is enough time in each week, month, and year to grow a joyful life. God outlines in the Bible how each particular relational garden can produce more love.

Through the Holy Spirit's whispers, we can feel encouraged to sow seeds of love, joy, peace, patience, kindness, goodness, gentleness, faithfulness, and self-control into our marriages, friendships, family, and so on. Then, when we do what He asks us to do, that part of our life will be very enjoyable and abundant. But if we neglect that relational garden or do things that damage it, we will be disappointed or attacked over time in that relational garden.

I want to say one thing about an "enemy" relationship, which is what happens if you and I have been takers or destroyers in one of the gardens. That relationship not only becomes barren, but also where that person or group is opposing you or rooting for you to fail for what you did to them or failed to do for them. Looking at the grid above, think about if there are gardens where an enemy relationship exists. Is your spouse an enemy? Are there members of your community that are enemies? What about colleagues? What about family members?

In the chart below, you can see that this person has turned their spouse into an enemy, some of their colleagues into enemies, and certain members of their community into enemies. The good news is that with God's help, the fruit of the Spirit can be cultivated in those areas making it possible to turn those enemies into good relationships once again. God promotes restoration and reconciliation in relationship; indeed, it is key to what He is all about (2 Cor 5:19).

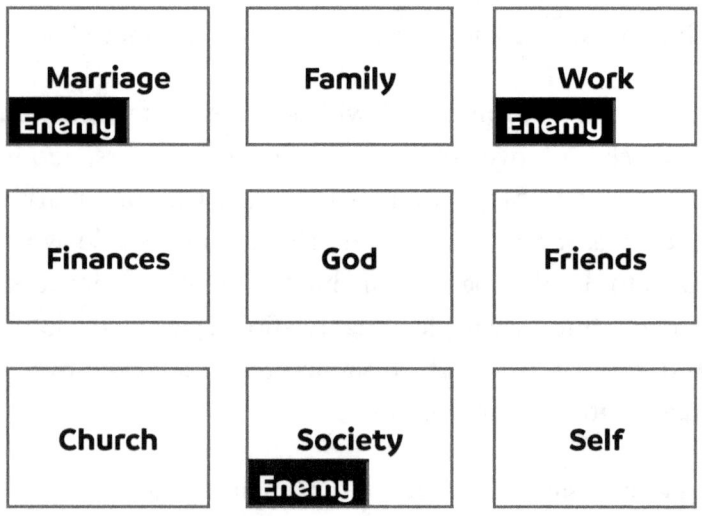

Too many of us have a mentality that someone else is responsible for us having a wonderful life. It is erroneous to think that we should just show up in our relationships and we will be showered with wonderful experiences, meaning, adoration, and the like. But this is not what the Scripture says. Galatians 6:7 says,

"Do not be deceived, God will not be mocked. Whatsoever a man sows that shall he also reap."

In other words, the quality of our relationships is dependent upon us partnering with God to grow that relationship to be all it can be. The following chart is meant to help you see what you may need to start doing to make a relationship better. Read the affirmations of the fruit of the Spirit, which states the actions of the fruit of the Spirit as a current reality. Ask God the Holy Spirit to guide you to the one you need to work on today. Which one(s) do you need to apologize for not pursuing?

Love:	Am I meeting the needs, pursuing, and pleasing the key people in my life?
Joy:	Am I positive and grateful, deepening my key relationships?
Peace:	Am I creating harmony, order, and calm wherever I go?
Patience:	Do I regularly give God and others more time?

Kindness: Am I pleasant, merciful, and encouraging?

Gentleness: Do I stay flexible and thoughtful when my expectations are not met?

Faithfulness: Do I trust God even if the path is difficult?

Self-Control: Do I moderate my desires to benefit others?

Remember, you are a relational gardener and Jesus wants to partner with you to have a delightful life full of true success. Listen for the whispers of His Spirit to add some more love, joy, peace, patience, and so forth into a particular relationship. Which garden does God want you to add love to today? Which one needs you to add patience? Which one needs your self-control?

3.
And the Greatest of These Is Love...

> *But the fruit of the Spirit is **love**, joy, peace, patience, kindness, goodness, gentleness, faithfulness, and self-control. (Gal 5:22,23)*

Recently, I have been very encouraged by the folks I have been asked to coach. The progress they have made with their pursuit, understanding, and listening to the whispers of God in this area of spiritual gardening has been incredible to hear about. God is clear in Matthew 22:37-39, Galatians 5:22,23,

www.ptlb.com/
grapeness-ch3

and John 15:1-10 that we are to allow Him to grow the fruit of the Spirit in and through our lives. One fruit is a mandatory requirement above all of the others for a relationship to grow—love. All of the various relational gardens need the aspects of love. None of them will prosper without it.

> *"There remain these three: faith, hope, and love, and the greatest of these is love."* (1 Cor 13:13)

The other day, I was talking with a man who recognized a new relational opportunity during time spent with his own mother. God was asking him to *grow love* in a part of his family garden that he had ignored for years. Due to a special set of events, God had put him and his mom together for more time than he was comfortable with, but he heard the whispers of God to love her. When he obeyed what God was telling him to do, this relational garden sprang to life with all kinds of blessings, interest, affection, and joy. He told me that instead of being upset about being "stuck" with his mom for four hours, he realized that God was giving him a chance to grow his garden. He just went with what God was prompting him to do, and it was a delightful time. Now, he might have been more interested in watching the games on the TV or spending time on some project at work or hanging out with friends or being with his immediate family, but he recognized that God had placed him with his mother, and she was a part of the family garden where he needed to grow love. This was a new orientation and reaction for him, and he found joy and blessing because of it.

Let's talk about what this looks like. How can you grow love in each of your relational gardens? First, know that this will look a little different in your marital/romantic garden, than it does in your family garden. Also demonstrating love at work will look differently than it does when you are spending time with God. Second, there are three underlying ideas that meet the definition of growing love in the various gardens—meet needs, pursue the soul, and please the other person.

God the Holy Spirit is speaking to us if we are willing to listen. How do we know His voice? When you receive a thought to sacrifice time or effort in order to meet your spouse's need, or to do homework with a child even though the game is on, that is God's whisper to you "to love" that person. Sometimes, we have an instinct or an intuition that we should sit and listen to a co-worker tell us about their difficulties, or help our son practice throwing the baseball. We don't know how we know to do this, but we somehow do. That is God's prompting for you to love. It is also like this little nudge to do something nice for your mom, spouse, or child—something that either meets a need, demonstrates pursuit of them, or something that will please them. Becoming sensitive to the Holy Spirit will push us into becoming a more loving, joyful, and peaceful person. We so often think we know what will build the best life, and so we set out to accomplish it, trampling over the people we will need if we get there. But the Holy Spirit whispers how to accomplish the grand plan He has for us and retain great relationships all along the journey.

I ask people I am coaching to make an affirmation for each one of the fruit of the Spirit. The first affirmation is this:

Love—I meet the needs, pursue the soul, and please the key people in my life.

This affirmation often shows you where God wants to do this in your life and where you are not doing this currently. God will prompt you to push into these elements of love in one or more of your gardens. Let's looks more closely at these aspects of love—meeting needs, pursuing the soul, and pleasing the other person.

Meeting Needs

The people who are important to you in your relational gardens have needs, and it is your job to meet those needs. What does it mean to meet the needs of another person? Sometimes their need is fairly obvious, such as providing a home or food, spending time with them, listening, giving hugs and giving them attention… Sometimes a person's needs are less obvious, like providing honesty, help, time alone, hope, correction, faith… God will prompt you to meet the needs of the other person. Sometimes these are things that may even be difficult or require sacrifice on your part, maybe some discomfort. Loving people in the way they need to be loved is not always easy.

The better we become at being sensitive to the relational needs of people, the clearer our assignments will become. Our society often wants to delegate too many of the essential tasks of a relationship. In the secular world this is called "relational skills," and it is handsomely rewarded. God the Holy Spirit wants to guide you to becoming a relational master.

Also, when God wants you to love the other person, He is sometimes asking you to look at the *long-term good* of the other person. I have talked to parents and spouses, who are dealing with addictions in their children or their marriage, and they have discovered that what their loved one needs is tough love, wake-up-call love, I-will-not-help-you-hurt-yourself-anymore love. Just remember that God is there for you to see it through.

Pursue the Soul

What does it mean to pursue the soul of the other person? We all have a mind, will, and set of emotions, which make up our soul. It is from our soul that our real life exists. We need for others to be interested in what we think, what we feel, and what we say. Sometimes the people in our relational gardens need to have someone care enough for someone to listen to what they are thinking at that moment, even if what they are saying makes no sense or is aimed in the complete wrong direction! To feel loved by someone else, we need to sense that they understand where we are coming from. That requires listening, asking questions, grappling with our perspective, and treating our ideas, emotions, and choices as serious. The same is true in reverse in order to show love to the other person. Sometimes when God is prompting you to love another person, it is this kind of love He is after—pursuit of their soul. When God wants me to pursue the soul of another person, I have the sense that I need to listen, and/or I need to let the other person explain himself or herself fully. To give people the gift of the pursuit of their soul is a very great thing. We cannot give this gift of listening and time to everyone, but we must give it to some. Even if you feel they need to change their mind about something, it starts from understanding where they are in the present moment. People are much more willing to listen and take advice when they feel understood; there is a sense of, "I can listen to you when I understand that you have truly understood what I think and feel."

I can remember when my youth pastor told me, "I don't think you love your mother."

"Of course I love my mother," I said.

"I want you to listen to your mother for one hour a day for three weeks," he said. That was a very tall order, and it would not be easy for me. But I was willing to hear the Lord's voice in the command of my youth pastor. I listened to my mother for one hour every day, and a great bond between my mom and I grew out of it. That is what pursuing the soul of another person looks like.

Years later, when I got married, I realized that the Lord was asking me to pursue the soul of my wife by listening to her for one hour every day. This simple habit of listening to my wife every day for an hour has created a delightful marriage and deep bond with this amazing woman. God the Holy Spirit will ask you to invest in certain people by listening to them and following their thoughts until you know them very well. This is the second aspect of what it means to love.

Please the Person

The third aspect of loving another person is to please another person. This doesn't mean to be immoral or go against our conscience or our sense of self, but it does mean that we understand the other person enough to do or say something that is truly a delight for the other person. It may be a foot massage or a date to their favorite Thai restaurant. It may be wearing a color they like or learning about a subject that the other person finds fascinating. The other person does not need this or even ask for it, but it is delightful to them. God sometimes will prompt you to delight the other person so that your relational garden can grow to its maximum. He knows that if all you do is meet needs, the spark of delight and joy may not be there. Delight them with something.

I never have to worry about God directing us to love people. He does this with promptings and whispers. I do have to worry that we will be too self-absorbed to listen or stubbornly refuse, because we don't want to sacrifice in the way God is suggesting. It is not always easy. It comes with sacrifice. It does not always "pay off" to love others, but do it anyway. It will enrich you personally.

You may get a prompting to call someone or send a note. You may get an urge to listen to a family member or a friend. You may strangely think of getting something for your spouse or for a co-worker even though it's not their birthday. These are all whispers from God to let Him grow love in your life. God is aware of what is needed and He wants you to live this amazing relational life. He must get us to act relationally with skill and abandonment. Only then can we truly enjoy life.

Jesus really does call us to a supernatural life where we let Him pour His love through us to others. It is quite a ride. I'll leave you with these two verses:

Jesus replied: "'Love the Lord your God with all your heart and with all your soul and with all your mind.' This is the first and greatest commandment. And the second is like it: 'Love your neighbor as yourself.' (Matt 22:37-39)

"The thief comes only to steal and kill and destroy; I have come that they may have life, and have it to the full." (John 10:10)

4.
Joy-Producing Positivity

*But the fruit of the Spirit is love, **joy**, peace, patience, kindness, goodness, gentleness, faithfulness, and self-control. (Gal 5:22,23)*

Do you agree that all of us would like to experience more joy in life? I do, and God calls us to rejoice in all things regardless of our circumstances (Phil 4:4). At times, I tend to notice everything bad about a situation, person, or relationship. My focus naturally goes to what needs improvement or is irritating to me about them. I am amused that God allows me to go all the way down this road where everything is bad and getting worse. It is then when He whispers to me, "Surely there

www.ptlb.com/
grapeness-ch4

are some things that are good and positive." When I am deep in my cynical view, I have a hard time thinking of anything good or positive. Slowly but surely God will get me to notice the good things in my life, in the country, in the church, in the people I know... Thankfully, I have learned to recognize God's call for me to notice the positive and the good as He whispers, "Be joyful."

One of my favorite verses on this subject is James 1:2–4.

> *"Consider it all joy my brethren when you encounter various trials knowing that the testing of your faith produces endurance. And let endurance have its perfect result that you may be perfect and complete, lacking in nothing."*

God will often bring this to my mind when I am sloughing through a list of things that have gone wrong or aren't working out the way I want them to. He is trying to get me to notice what is right, good, positive, and encouraging. He is developing me, strengthening me, and completing me. The more I look with Him, the more I am able to see positive people, positive and encouraging outcomes, and positive elements all around me. If I put all my focus on the positive, a new level of joy springs up in my life.

Since God wants to grow joy in our lives, He will ask us to do certain things to increase our joy so that we can enjoy others and have others enjoy us as well. If we were willing to admit it, sometimes we are not much fun to be around. Change that and choose joy.

Joy-Producing Positivity

How does God go about increasing our joy? I believe He does it by focusing our gaze, our attention, on the good things about people and circumstances. Everybody we meet is an amalgam of good, bad, weaknesses, strengths, negatives, and positives. In order to have joy, we have to narrow our focus on the good, the positives, and the strengths. Think about it. If you go to a football game and your favorite team is winning, but you can't escape the knowledge that there are people being hurt, oppressed, and wounded all over the world, you would not be able to enjoy your time at the game, right? That's because your focus is too broad. If you are going to take delight and joy in anything, you have to segment the positive from out of the sinful world in which we live. In other words, in order to grow joy in your life, God will ask you to focus on good times and good qualities to overcome the pain and evil around you.

The word *joy* is the word *chara* in the Greek, which means *gladness, delight, joy*. There is an element of *positivity* in this word. To raise your joy level, God the Holy Spirit may have you focus on a sliver of your world. It may be something positive about a particular person; something positive about a particular situation; something positive about a particular relationship. That particular thing may be the only positive, joy-producing part of that person or relationship, but God wants you to focus there. He wants you to find delight in that small thing so that you can expand the joy to the whole of the person.

This is tough to do with a difficult person. Our natural tendency is to notice the wrong within a person, a relationship, or a situation. We think, "It is so obvious to us, so why aren't they doing something about that?" But very few people respond well to the critic—the person who comes to tell us what we are doing wrong is not well received, generally. All of us respond positively to the person who tells us what we are doing right, right? We all seem to have an innate sense of what we are doing well, and we want others to notice it also. When a person notices our strengths, our positive behaviors, or our sacrificial actions, then we are able to receive a little corrective criticism from them from time to time.

I can remember what a powerful difference this made in a number of my relationships. I had always been quick to spot the things that needed to be changed, the things that were wrong. I didn't have any trouble pointing out what they were. But instead of going right to those things that needed to be fixed (in my mind), I communicated the things that were right about the person, about the situation, about the relationship. When I did this, the other person brightened and opened up their friendly side to me.

During a specific time when I was praying through the fruit of the Spirit, God just whispered the word *joy*. I asked, "Who?" and He immediately brought one of my daughters to mind. She was going through a lot of emotional turmoil at the time, and I realized that God wanted me to spend some more time with her rehearsing how wonderful she was. I spent time the rest of that day thinking of all of her strengths, positives, and good decisions. I sat her down when I made it home to let her know all of these positives that I knew were true of her. As you can imagine, she was very encouraged by this listing of her positive qualities. My actions brought more joy to her and to our relationship.

I watch in horror sometimes as parents, spouses, and bosses rehearse over and over what irritates them about the other person. *This produces the opposite of joy.* If, instead, we ask God to remind us of the positives about this person, we would experience joy.

God the Holy Spirit wants you to focus on what is good, right, and positive about a person. Listen to those promptings. Some may say that it is unrealistic to focus so narrowly on the good within a person without seeing the whole picture of who they are at the same time. But this overall view always diminishes the joy one person has with another. So, focus your mind on the good things in your life.

God's Recipe for Joy

Look at the admonition in Philippians 4:8.

> *"Finally brethren, whatever is true, whatever is honorable, whatever is right, whatever is pure, whatever is lovely, whatever is of good repute, if there is any excellence and if anything is worthy of praise, dwell on these things."*

Or, James 1:2–4.

"Consider it all joy my brethren when you encounter various trials, knowing that the testing of your faith produces endurance. And let endurance have its perfect result that you may be perfect and complete, lacking in nothing."

To increase the level of joy in your life, do these few things:

1. Memorize these two verses above repeating them slowly as you go to sleep tonight. Let the grace and joy of these verses fill your soul while you are sleeping.

2. What or who in particular is God focusing you on that brings joy or delight, or who needs some positivity?

3. Consider what is good about the situation or what the person does well. What have they done that is very beneficial? What are three situations they excel at? Then determine how can you focus on those areas.

4. When you apply Philippians 4:8 to the person or situation, notice your level of joy increasing. Give thanks to God for the joy-filled moment.

5. In what ways is God sending you trials to make you a better person, and where are the elements of positive and good in the midst of this difficulty?

Heed the elements of joy that God whispers to your heart. As you do, may you be made perfect and lacking in nothing.

5.
Bringing Harmony, Order, and Calm—Peace

> But the fruit of the Spirit is love, joy, **peace**, patience, kindness, goodness, gentleness, faithfulness, and self-control. (Gal 5:22,23)

Jesus' direct comments from Matthew 22:37-39 help us understand that the proper goal for successful life is relational. It's not material, power-based, or hedonistic. He has given us two key gifts to help build great relationships. One is the Scriptures that give us key pieces of relational "codes"

www.ptlb.com/
grapeness-ch5

to insert into our various relationships to make them healthy, loving, and delightful. The second is the Holy Spirit, who whispers, urges, and prompts the right times and situations in which to introduce various new relational actions, words, emotions, and attitudes for deeply enjoyable relationships.

Building great relationships requires the ability to bring peace to a dramatic situation or a flailing organization, or even to someone who is stressed, angry, or upset. In fact, a great relationship cannot be built without peace. God calls us to be peacemakers knowing that this is one of the keys to a blessed life:

> "Blessed are the peacemakers, for they shall be called sons of God." (Matt 5:9)

The Scriptures tell us that God the Holy Spirit will whisper to us at crucial moments when to inject the relational codes for peace into our lives. We have to be prepared for these whispers and recognize God's role in placing them in our minds for us to act upon. The elements of peace are often ideas that we would not think up on our own, and they may even run counter to our natural inclinations. There are three general elements that produce peace: harmony, order, and calm.

Harmony

Creating harmony in a relationship is the idea of moving in concert or connection with another person, like dancing in sync with the people in your life to promote agreement and unity. Harmony is often disrupted when everyone wants to do things their own way or not participate with a spirit of cooperation, as is the case when there are too many leaders and no followers. In my life, I always want to lead, but that is not how real life works. In order to have real relationships with real people, I need to let them lead sometimes. I need to allow them to set the melody, the tempo, the key, and the steps. Often our lack of peace in relationships is due to the fact that we only want to dance to the topics we pick, activities that interest us, people we are drawn toward, purchases that we like, and situations that suit us. Certainly there are times when we do need to lead, but not always; we must come to realize the unique delights and perspectives that come from allowing the people we are in relationship with to lead. If I am going to have a real relationship with my co-workers, my friends, my children, my parents, or my spouse, then I must hear what they are saying and understand what they want to do. At times, I need to let them lead in the dance of our relationship.

Order

Creating order in relationships is the idea of organizing its structure in a particular way. I am amazed at the number of people who want peace in their family but are unwilling to bring any kind of order to it. If there are no rules, plans, rituals, manners, and elements of respect, nor responsibilities for each person in a family, then there will never be peace. Peace demands structure and predictability. There will always be opportunities for change but relationships can't be structureless. Not everyone in the family gets to say what happens, or at least it shouldn't be that way. In every great relationship, there must be structure, leaders, respect, duties, consequences, and celebrations. It seems recently I have been interacting with people on a weekly basis, who are trying to have a great family or a great marriage or a great work place but with no structure or order. It just can't happen. God the Holy Spirit may whisper to you that you can bring peace to the situation (to your own soul) by being an active agent in bringing order. Maybe you need to lead; maybe you need to follow; maybe you need to suggest structures; maybe you need to introduce manners and respect... just realize that whatever the Holy Spirit urges you to do may be a key element in the future peace or strife that this relationship will enjoy or endure.

Realize, too, that if the present structure, or lack of it, is not working, then God the Holy Spirit will prompt you to act in some way to bring order and peace to the situation. I must tell you that many times when there is a lack of peace in a relationship, I immediately think of "my solution" to the lack-of-order problem. If everyone just did it "my way," then we would have peace! I have found that God the Holy Spirit does not think the same way that I do. His still, small voice looks at the whole situation and whispers different things other than "demand your way." He has suggested to me that I read certain books or articles, that I really listen to what the other person(s) is saying, or that the solution will appear in some other way. Many times, I have also found that God the Holy Spirit prompts me to be a part of building peace in the relationship instead of expecting instant peace. He wants the relationship to grow into one of peace and order.

Calm

The concept of calm in a relationship is about controlling our emotions and reactions in such a way as to promote peace, tranquility, and a trouble-free atmosphere. In order to have calm, we cannot let our emotional reactions to a person or situation spill out in such a way that the whole relationship is disturbed, damaged, or even destroyed. Yes, there are lots of things that can happen to upset a relationship; perhaps your relational partner did something that changes the future that was planned, or someone said something very harmful or upsetting to you. We can be tempted to lose our temper or fly into a series of actions that are based upon what we know at that moment, but God usually asks us to process our reactions in a calm manner so that our emotions don't blow up the relationship. Relationships can die because of the actions of others and our own actions, but they should not die because of our reactions.

When it comes to rumor or gossip or slander, the Holy Spirit will whisper to us that we need to deal with reality and what really happened, not just react to what we heard from someone else. It is possible that what someone is telling you is actually what the person did or said, but it is also possible that it is not. Get the facts. Let the Holy Spirit give you a calm exterior as you gather the facts of a situation, which usually requires confronting the person directly—in a calm way. We want to avoid looking foolish when all the facts are in.

Become a Peacemaker

God wants to produce peace through your life using words, actions, emotions, and attitudes that are designed to bring harmony between people, order in a relationship, and calm to situations. As peacemakers, He wants to use you to do it. You can train yourself to be alert to His promptings, urges, and whispers. You can achieve peace in a number of ways, but it might look something like this:

- Saying nothing but doing something.
- Saying something bold.
- A change in your attitude (your mental perspective) and acting from that new angle.
- Keeping your emotions in check outwardly even though they may be raging on the inside.

Whatever He chooses to do, remember He wants to use you to change the dynamics in the relationship towards peace. In most cases, He is not going to send an invisible spirit of peace to calm the other person down or change their mind, although He has done this before (1 Chron 12:18). Because of Jesus Christ, He has already sent the Spirit of Peace *to reside in believers, which means you, if you have received Him as your Lord and Savior.* The Spirit of Christ wants to teach you to behave differently in order to spark a change in behavior in everybody else. Too often we want God to be like a super hero, who fires invisible rays of peace from a cannon directed at the other person so that they will change. But, that's not how He works. Instead, He wants to whisper to you how to be the peace-giving device in the situation instead of continuing to fight for your point of view.

Let me add that the relational codes for peace are both short-term and long-term oriented. In some cases, His codes will bring immediate peace to a tense situation, while in other situations, they move the relationship slowly to a place where there is less tension and strife. Be ready for both kinds of whispers from God, both long-term and short-term solutions.

Apology Process

When there is a lack of peace in one of my relationships, God consistently whispers to me to look for something I have done to wound the other person. Often times, we inadvertently offend the other person not realizing that we have done something wrong. Most people are not pleased to be in a relationship with an offensive person! If I notice something I've done, then I apologize and ask for forgiveness. Years ago, I learned an effective apology process taught to me by a trusted mentor that I still follow to this day. When I am the cause of the lack of harmony, I do these things to bring about reconciliation and peace. It involves six key steps:

Step One: Become gentle in your approach and manner. An aggressive or arrogant apology will not work. *"A gentle answer turns away wrath, but a harsh word stirs up anger."* (Prov. 15:1)

Step Two: Seek education. *"So watch yourselves. 'If your brother or sister sins against you, rebuke them; and if they repent, forgive them.'"* (Luke 17:3)

This means that you must understand the nature of your offense from the other person's point of view. You might say, "I know that I have offended you, but I am not even sure of all the ways that I wounded you. I don't want to hurt you, so would you help me understand how I hurt you?" It can be very hard to hear their response, but it is crucial to you growing and learning from your actions. Do not try and defend yourself; just listen with receptivity to what the other person is saying.

If, after you have listened, you find there was a misunderstanding about certain facts, you can gently bring those up, but not to defend yourself—just work towards bringing accuracy to their understanding. Most people try to defend themselves, and it wrecks the apology. Don't defend; just clarify if it is helpful. Don't talk about your intentions or someone else's fault; just seek to understand their perspective.

Step Three: Admit you were wrong. *"Never pay back evil for evil to anyone. Respect what is right in the sight of all men. If possible, so far as it depends on you, be at peace with all men."* (Rom 12:17,18)

After you have heard why they are wounded, admit you were wrong for offending and wounding them. You may feel like they are focused on only five percent of what actually happened, instead of the eighty or ninety percent of what was really going on. But they need a sense that you understood what you did and an admission of guilt for the part they are focused on. I remember one time I was talking with a person who was offended with how aggressive and powerful I had said something to them. What I said was the truth, but they were offended and wounded by my manner and tone. I needed to hear their pain and apologize or else the relationship was not going to go forward. "Yes, you're right," I said. "I should have spoken to you in a different manner. I was wrong."

Step Four: Ask for forgiveness. *"So watch yourselves. 'If your brother or sister sins against you, rebuke them; and if they repent, forgive them.'"* (Luke 17:3)

Ask the person to forgive you and wait for a "yes" answer. It is important for the person to say the words, "Yes, I forgive you." And, it is important for you to hear that they do forgive you. If they cannot forgive you at that moment, then the relationship is at a stand still. It takes two people to have a relationship, and either one or both parties cannot be harboring things that are not forgiven. It will be a block for moving forward.

Step Five: Devise a repentance plan.

If the wound is deep or a repeated offense, then it may be important to develop a repentance plan for the next time you commit the wound again. Repentance plans are sort of like fences or boundaries that come with consequences to keep you from doing the offense again. I remember one husband, who would watch a sports program with his boys every Saturday. He and his boys would make great sandwiches in the kitchen, but would consistently leave the kitchen a mess as they rushed out to watch the program. This was a constant wound to the wife and mom, because her thinking was that the "boys" thought so little of her as evidenced by their leaving the kitchen a mess. Week after week this continued with no resolution, even though he apologized. But the next week he would always forget. In order to try and convey how he truly understood that this was an issue in the relationship, he offered up a repentance plan if he messed up again. He would clean up all the Sunday dishes if he forgot again. He hated doing the dishes, and he only had to "forget" three times before he learned to remember. The point is that he cared enough to correct his behavior, even if it meant enduring the penalty to finally get it right.

Step Six: Test for openness.

Testing for openness is paramount to making sure the apology is genuinely received. It may be that your first apology worked the first time; you'll know this because the other person is open to relationship with you as you go forward. If you ask them a question about something else, they are open to talking. In the case of your spouse, if you want to hug them as a gesture of peace, it will be allowed. If you test for openness and there is still mistrust and a closed reaction, then you may not have worked through all the issues. If they won't forgive, then there is something else there—another offense that has yet to be spoken. They do not believe you are sincere and are not ready to stop resenting you for what you did. When I get to this place and there is still a closed reaction after my apology, I go back to step one and start again. It is better to spend an hour doing an apology right, than enduring three weeks of anger and distance in the relationship.

The Peace of Christ

As the giver and source of peace, God has a lot to say about peace and peace making in the scriptures. Read and learn from these various Scriptures. Let God give you wisdom about peace through reading and rereading these verses, as well as the verses above.

> "Peace I leave with you; My peace I give to you; not as the world gives do I give to you. Do not let your heart be troubled, nor let it be fearful." (John 14:27)

> "Let no unwholesome word proceed from your mouth, but only such a word as is good for edification according to the need of the moment, so that it will give grace to those who hear. Do not grieve the Holy Spirit of God, by whom you were sealed for the day of redemption. Let all bitterness and wrath and anger and clamor and slander be put away from you, along with all malice. Be kind to one another, tender-hearted, forgiving each other, just as God in Christ also has forgiven you. Therefore be imitators of God, as beloved children; and walk in love,

just as Christ also loved you and gave Himself up for us, an offering, and a sacrifice to God as a fragrant aroma." (Eph 4:29-5:2)

"And the peace of God, which surpasses all comprehension, will guard your hearts and your minds in Christ Jesus. Finally, brethren, whatever is true, whatever is honorable, whatever is right, whatever is pure, whatever is lovely, whatever is of good repute, if there is any excellence and if anything is worthy of praise, dwell on these things. The things you have learned and received and heard and seen in me, practice these things, and the God of peace will be with you." (Phil 4:7-9)

6.
Giving Room and Time for Change—Patience

*But the fruit of the Spirit is love, joy, peace, **patience**, kindness, goodness, gentleness, faithfulness, and self-control. (Gal 5:22,23)*

The other day, I was having a wonderful time praying and interacting with God. The focus shifted to how long it has taken God to bring me to the place I am now. I am not perfect by any stretch, but I am very different from who I was twenty years ago, ten years ago, or even five years ago. God has

www.ptlb.com/
grapeness-ch6

patiently worked with me to be wiser, more knowledgeable, and more understanding of how the world really works. Sure, I have said and done things that were immature, foolish, or just plain wrong in the past, but He did not reject me or give up on me. He pointed out to me how He has put up with my bad attitudes, selfishness, and wrong priorities, all the while still loving me towards this day when I am much better and our relationship is incredible.

All this time, God has been playing the long game with me—growing me, molding me, preparing me for this life (Eph 2:10). Long ago, He could see what I could become and what our relationship could become. He did not feel the need to point out all my flaws, then or now. He just continues to love me and celebrates each new insight I gain (that He already knew) and each new step of growth towards becoming a better, more loving person. He feels the same way about you.

When I am patient with people in my life, *I give God, myself, and the other person time to change in order to make the relationship better.* I see how important patience is and remains to be valuable in each of my relationships. There will always be things that can change to make a relationship better. When God the Holy Spirit prompts *patience*, He is saying that we need to give Him, ourselves, or the other person time to grow and mature. What irritates us is not that big a deal in the grand scheme of things, really. We've all done things that irritate others.

This need for patience is true in each relationship. There will be things that irritate and frustrate you about the other person(s), because they are not, nor will they ever be, perfect on this side of eternity. We tend to think, "If only they would be this way; if only they would do that, then the relationship would be so much better." "I can hardly stand to be with them, because they just keep doing that thing that bugs me!" But God is saying that if you only focus on the thing that bugs you, it could severely damage your relationship. That is why we need patience.

One of the things that my wife, Dana, and I do when we are irritated or frustrated by the other is to wait two hours and/or two days to bring it up to see if we can still remember what we were so irritated about. Most of the time we can't even remember what had us all worked up; we can remember being irritated, but not what we were irritated about.

The Long Game—Long-Suffering

In every relationship, there are good, bad, irritating, and delightful elements. We revel in the good and delightful ones, and we always want to change the bad or irritating elements. Usually we want the rough places of a relationship to change right away, but that is not often possible. When that happens, God asks us for a longer, enduring patience. He asks us to play the long game. This makes sense given that God Himself is longsuffering. Look at what these Scriptures tell us about His level of patience:

*"The Lord, The Lord God, compassionate and gracious, **slow to anger**, and abounding in loving-kindness and truth;" (Ex 34:7)*

*"Or do you show contempt for the riches of his kindness, **forbearance and patience**, not realizing that God's kindness is intended to lead you to repentance?" (Rom 2:4)*

*"The Lord is **longsuffering** and abundant in mercy, forgiving iniquity and transgression; but He by no means clears the guilty, visiting the iniquity of the fathers on the children to the third and fourth generation." (Num 14:18) (NKJV)*

*"But you, Lord, are a compassionate and gracious God, **slow to anger**, abounding in love and faithfulness." (Ps 86:15)*

Sometimes I believe what God is asking us to do when He whispers *patience* is to take the long view—to think one year out, five years out, ten years out, or longer. He asks us to consider, "How could I bring about a change in that irritating or bad thing over time?" "How could I cooperate with God so that the irritating or bad element would change or be removed at some point in the future?" "What forms of encouragement, experiences, or education could I introduce over the next five years to change the situation?"

Too often, we want to just confront a person with the things that we find unpleasant about them. We want to say,

Giving Room and Time for Change—Patience

"Please change this right now!" But usually that will causes a huge fight and resistance. When God prompts us to be patient, He is asking us to allow Him, others, and even ourselves to have more time to bring about a needed change. I talk with parents all the time who want their children to change, but they are trying to promote change too quickly. Most of us change in five-year-time periods. Think about bringing about change and a different relationship at the end of five years.

I have heard the Lord whisper to me about being patient in all my relationships. What He is really telling me is, "Let the relationship grow over time." "Would you allow that irritating thing to change without talking about it?" "In what ways could you positively encourage the relationship so that the irritating thing would disappear over the next five years?"

There have been things that I had planned to talk with my wife and my daughters about fifteen years in the future, because I knew at the time they could not handle me talking about those issues at that moment. There were some really important ones that God has reminded me about all these years later, and the discussions went so much differently than they would have if I had spoken out at the earlier time. God will prompt us to exercise His patience so that the relationship can grow. We have to realize that the relationship is more important than some petty irritation or frustration.

Think about how God deals with us. He takes the long game and only asks us to present to Him a heart of wisdom by the end of our life (Ps 90:12). In other words, He asks us to grow into a better person over the course of our lives. He asks us to be in relationship with Him (Matt 22:37-39), and yet, He does not immediately confront us with all of the things that irritate Him about us. He works with us *over time*. God is steering, guiding, and directing us for our own benefit and the benefit of our relationship with Him. He steers us into an area of relational growth through a seminar, or causes us to notice a book, or promotes engagement with a new person who grows us up in some way. He has a "place" where He wants us to be in five years, and He is giving us every opportunity to get there. He does, at times, demand us to change in some arena more quickly, but that is not the regular nature of our relationship with Him. He is patient.

I know that my wife has been waiting for years and decades for me to realize certain things about myself that will allow me to be better and our relationship to improve. I am just now catching up to her wisdom and patience! There have been conversations that I have waited fifteen years to have with my children, and when they finally came about, it was delightful and very helpful for them and me. We have become way too immediate in our relationships, expecting too much too fast, and it is costing us greatly.

I hear more and more people saying things like… "I just can't put up with a person who does this or that." I wonder whether our growing ability to declare very specifically our wants and desires has contributed to the number of people who live alone? I do not advocate that we put up with immorality or violence, but I do think that every relationship involves an imperfect person, and therefore, all our relationships need patience.

Active versus Passive

Let me finish by saying that this is not a passive kind of patience, just as God's patience with us is not passive. This spirit-led patience is active and seeks the best for the other person. It is willing to push towards that goal for years. I am always actively arranging conversations, growth opportunities, new people, seminars, praise, and encouragement for steps toward a better relationship. Patience is not passive, but it lengthens the timeline and is willing to move more slowly, almost unperceptively, toward a beneficial goal.

When God whispers *patience* in your soul, it is usually about something that is irritating in a relationship. What is God prompting you to be patient about? What is He prompting you to attack in a very patient five- to fifteen-year plan rather than a right-now confrontation? Ask yourself how could you change the relationship over five to fifteen years, and what it could look like in five to fifteen years from now? Pray like mad that you recognize all the subtle things you could do that would bring about the changes over the course of those years. Patience is a good thing; God uses it on us and aren't you glad? Let God prompt you to be patient. Your relationships will be better.

> "The end of a matter is better than its beginning; Patience of spirit is better than haughtiness of spirit." (Ecc 7:8)

"So, as those who have been chosen of God, holy and beloved, put on a heart of compassion, kindness, humility, gentleness and patience;" (Col 3:12)

7.
The Pleasant Helpfulness of Kindness

> But the fruit of the Spirit is love, joy, peace, patience, **kindness**, goodness, gentleness, faithfulness, and self-control. (Gal 5:22,23)

Whenever I am talking with someone for any extended period of time, I find myself asking the Holy Spirit which of the fruit of the Spirit He wants me to give that person. It is a simple exercise really, as I listen to the whispers of God while I continue to interact with the other person. This way

www.ptlb.com/grapeness-ch7

of letting God flow through me jumped out to me when I was talking with a young lady at church the other day. Normally this woman asks for help and the usual message from the Lord is to benefit her in they way she is asking (that is goodness in the list of the fruit of the Spirit). But this time, as I was talking with her, I just kept hearing kindness. So, I tried to be as pleasant as I could and encouraged her from the position of pleasant encouragement. I could tell in just a few minutes that really what she needed was to talk to someone who was positive and encouraging. It was great to be an agent of God in this woman's life—God streamed through me what she needed at that moment.

We have been learning in this book that God the Holy Spirit wants to move in and through us to build our relationships into great ones via ways that are hard or impossible for us to do naturally. He wants us to have the best possible relationships so He prompts us to:

- Meet needs, pursue a soul, and please another. *(love)*

- Focus on the positive instead of the negative in a situation. *(joy)*

- Bring order, calm, and harmony to a relationship. *(peace)*

- Be willing to work for the long-term goal. *(patience)*

- Treat people in a way that is better than they deserve – a pleasant helpfulness. *(kindness)*

Yes, this last bullet point is the definition of *kindness*, our next fruit of the Spirit. The Greek word is *chrestotes*, which is most often translated *kindness*. But most people don't truly know what kindness is. In order to understand kindness, one needs to look at two words in the New Testament—*mercy and grace*.

- To receive mercy means to receive less than we deserve.

- To receive grace means that we receive far more than we deserve.

Kindness vs. Goodness

The two words in the fruit of the Spirit verse, kindness and goodness, have this opposite quality. For a person to be kind means that we treat people with a pleasant helpfulness that is much more merciful than justice or fairness would demand. To exercise goodness means that we benefit people more than they deserve. Focusing on this idea of kindness, there will constantly be people in your life who do you wrong or treat you unfairly, and God will often prompt you to treat them with a pleasant helpfulness that they do not deserve.

I can think of many marriages that have been destroyed because one or both spouses treat each other with a level of venom that the other person's actions, mistakes, and offenses deserve. But a great marriage cannot be built in this world on strict justice. A great marriage demands kindness. Neither can a family survive on strict justice. If parents do not offer more encouragement than their children deserve, then the children will be crippled in reaching their full potential and enjoying their family. If children demand that their parents be perfect in behavior and parenting skills, then rebellion, distrust, and hatred will inevitably follow. *Kindness is required for good relationships.*

What Does Extending Kindness Look Like?

To have good, healthy relationships means that one or both people in a relationship practices kindness. Nor do they require strict accounting for every wrong inflicted. First Corinthians 13 says that love does not take into account a wrong suffered… it bears all things, believes all things, hopes all things, endures all things. This is a higher kind of love—God's recipe for love.

I get the benefit of a wonderful marriage because my wife is so kind to me. She does not treat me as I often deserve. Instead, she offers a pleasant helpfulness towards me. Yes, there are times when she corrects me and requests that I apologize for certain things, but the general tenor of her actions towards me are a pleasant helpfulness that I do not deserve (but am all too glad to accept).

My children know that their father is not perfect. They know that I love them and am doing the best I can to raise them right and treat them fairly. They extend to me a pleasant helpfulness—a kindness that I don't necessarily deserve, and thus our relationship flourishes. I also extend to them kindness—a pleasant helpfulness that allows them to make mistakes, to develop, to choose a path different than mine, to be less than perfect, while still receiving my love, encouragement, and overwhelming support. Our relationship is strong and delightful because of the kindness they extend to me in not remembering the times when I got angry or made a bad decision or failed to be perfect. And also, because I offer them kindness to not remember all that they said when they were mad at me, or the times when I was right and they were wrong. Relationships need kindness or they will die.

Life is messy and filled with difficult people; some live in our own immediate or extended families. (And sometimes that difficult person is you!) Yes, there are people who will take advantage of our kindness, and there will be times when God does not suggest that kindness is what that relationship needs. He may instead prompt us to offer some tough love to the selfish taker, but generally kindness is so often needed if a relationship is to survive. This is true of the relationships at work, at church, in the neighborhood, and all over our lives. Without the milk of kindness, we won't have any relationships—only transactions.

There have been times when I have been really upset at my wife over this or that. I have wanted to give her a piece of my mind about how much her actions or inactions hurt me or changed my plans. I can remember times trying to pray about these offenses and asking God to help me make it clear that I was not going to put up with this kind of behavior. Each time

I did that, God prompted me to be kind. He prompted me to treat her in a way that she clearly did not deserve.

I remember one time I was so upset and was just waiting for her to come home to unload my wounds, but God suggested that I go to the store and get her a gift at a store she liked! I was aghast at that idea that obviously did not come from me, and I began arguing with God. *That will not teach her the right lesson, I thought.* But God just kept on prompting until I took the girls and we went to the store and bought mom a gift—we had it wrapped and everything. We all got so excited about mom seeing the gift and opening it. We put it right in the path when she came into the house. It was the most amazing thing—I actually became more excited about how encouraged she would be with the gift than making my point! God's prompting of kindness did more to improve the atmosphere in my marriage that night than a million words of hurt, anger, or frustration.

The key to being great in God's kingdom is to be the servant of the Lord to other people. God will often suggest that you offer pleasant helpfulness to someone who doesn't deserve it so that you can build a better relationship with that person, but He might suggest other fruits as well. Ask God to show you what fruit of the Spirit the people around you need. Listen to the whispers of the Holy Spirit and do what He suggests, letting Him flow through you to them. His instructions will lead to a much better result than the ideas you come up with on your own. You will be amazed at how people respond. He knows what He's talking about. You can trust Him!

8.
Doing More Than They Truly Deserve— Goodness

*But the fruit of the Spirit is love, joy, peace, patience, kindness, **goodness**, gentleness, faithfulness, and self-control. (Gal 5:22,23)*

One of the joys of being a Christian is when God the Holy Spirit prompts us to do things that we would not even think to do but are crucial for others and us to keep growing.

www.ptlb.com/
grapeness-ch8

Before we jump into the next ingredient for strong relationships, goodness, let's do a little review. Remember that we all have nine basic relationships to foster in life, as indicated in the chart below.

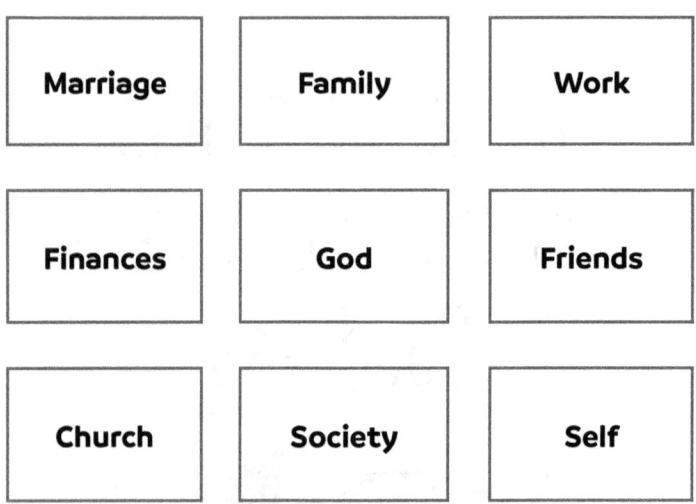

There are some basic truths I want to highlight about these relationships:

1. Each relationship consists of someone independent of the other relationships in your life, so success in one doesn't mean success in all. In other words, I can have a flourishing relationship with my children, while I am not doing very well with the people at work. The goal is to have success at some level in all of them.

2. Each relationship has boundaries for growing that relationship. Those boundaries could be roughly seen as the Ten Commandments, which can be equated to

God's guide for how to treat others. Behaviors that would require me to violate the Ten Commandments in a relational area are not healthy and should not be permitted. This is a foundational truth for all relationships.

3. The basic construction materials in each relationship begin with the fruit of the Spirit: love, joy, peace, patience, kindness, goodness, gentleness, faithfulness, and self-control. There are other relational building materials as well, but if you just used liberal amounts of these in each relationship, you would come out all right.

4. Each relationship requires a unique version of the fruit of the Spirit that is appropriate for that relationship. For example, the type of love needed (meeting needs, pursuing the soul, and pleasing) will be different in my marriage than it will be with my colleagues at work.

Defining Goodness

The sixth element in the fruit of the Spirit, *goodness*, is an also expression of love, but it is a unique and distinct thing. Much like kindness, every thriving relationship needs it. The word *goodness* is the Greek word *agathosune*, which means *to benefit another; to do for another what they do not deserve; to benefit them in some way*. This means that there are times when God will whisper to us to do something, say something, provide something, or in some way benefit another person. I find that

I am not usually aware of what the benefit is until God clearly says, "Do this."

The other day I was standing in line at lunch waiting to pay for my food. The lady ahead of me was paying for her meal and heading to the drinks, napkins, and forks area. While I was paying, one of the servers behind the counter ran over to the lady who had just paid and must have said that her card did not go through because the lady gave them her card again. By the time I made it to the drinks, napkins, and forks area, the server was back with the bad news—the card did not work again. The lady did not have another card, and so I heard her say, "Well, you just have to take it back I guess!" Right then is when I heard the whisper of the Holy Spirit, "Pay for her meal." I looked at the situation again, and again I heard that whisper, "Pay for her meal." So I did. I walked back and gave the person behind the counter my card and had them scan it for her meal. Then they brought the lady's meal back to her. It was delightful to be in the midst of a Holy Spirit transaction. I was God's servant in that moment and had benefitted this lady that I did not even know. This is what it means to be good—doing something that truly benefits someone else. It can be a person you know or a stranger, as it was in this case. When we are filled with the Holy Spirit, we are open to His promptings to do something good for others.

God tells us that a great life is one filled with great relationships (Matt 22:37-39), which means that we must be open to God's direction to do good for others. God has assignments that He wants us to do that will benefit others

Doing More Than They Truly Deserve—Goodness

and keep us open to Him. There are all kinds of people we come in contact with each day, and each of them is on their own pathway. God is fully aware of what is happening to each of these people and when they need to be truly benefitted in some way to keep them on their path. Sometimes He chooses to use you as the key delivery agent for the benefit that the other person needs. It might be financial. Your action could be listening. God may want you to help them move or tell them how to solve a problem. It is different every time, tailored to fit the person and their need. As God keeps track of everyone's life, He knows what they need and that He has you, His agent, nearby to deliver the need. Most often we are asked by God to deliver a much-needed benefit to those we know the most, but sometimes God has a unique assignment for us.

Our ability to hear God's goodness assignments begins with our relationship with Him, which He provided for us to have by the life, death, and resurrection of Jesus Christ. This relationship continues to grow and blossom as we learn how to build and grow the other relationships in our life God's way within our own unique context. God supplies all we need to have great relationships; we just need to do the work of putting them into our lives as He prompts us.

A few years back, I was at a bike shop getting my bike fixed and retrofitted for me in some new ways. While I was there, I was drawn to a particular bike that was marked fifty percent off. It was a big bike, too big for me, and I remember letting the Lord know that it was too big for me. He whispered that it was not for me but for another person, a very big guy. I realized then that God had supplied the money, and I was supposed to give it to a young man I knew. What a delight! I purchased the bike and told the bike shop that the fellow would be by in the next couple of weeks to pick it up. Then I had the exciting opportunity to tell the young man that there was a brand new bike at the bike shop waiting for him with his name on it—one that had been specifically designed for a person of his height. He went in and picked it up, and he used the bike to exercise and reduce the wear and tear on the family car. It was very exciting to be a part of this blessing to him and his family.

In relationships, it is often true that we can fall into a tit-for-tat arrangement. You did this for me, so I will do that for you; or, I will do this for you in hopes that you will do that for me. The Holy Spirit wants to break up this type of small thinking. He wants us to truly benefit others in ways that they don't expect. Think back in your life to those people or situations where God sent you someone who was truly a blessing or they did something that was amazing for you. That is the kind of God we serve.

As we saw in our last chapter on kindness, kindness is often about doing less than a person deserves or being merciful. Goodness is like grace, and we are to do more for the other person than they deserve. God has introduced us into His grace, where we receive far more from Him than we deserve. It is this same idea that is contained in goodness when God the Holy Spirit prompts us to be good to others. Are you open to God being lavish and extravagant to another person through you? God is the God of the Universe, and we are often scrimping and saving money like He will run out. God was extravagant when He sent His own son to die for us. I know that He wants to show through us that He is still that same lavish and amazingly gracious God. If you are open to the whispers of God, you will hear Him suggest to truly benefit another person way beyond what they deserve.

I have a friend who regularly gives waitresses a $20 tip on a $20 meal. He received a prompting from the Lord, who wants him to be as extravagant with goodness to the waitress as God has been with Him. Another friend of mine noticed a woman on a corner, who was holding a sign asking for help. She was clearly pregnant and looked pretty helpless. Not sure of whether this was a scam or not, she wasn't inclined to do anything to help her. But the Lord prompted my friend to purchase a grocery card from a nearby store and give it to the woman. She obeyed, albeit reluctantly. She figured that the Lord knew what He was doing. The woman seemed very surprised and very grateful, but that wasn't the best part. After my friend gave her the card, she also gave her a big hug. The woman was grateful for the gift, but with tears in her eyes, she said she was even more grateful for the hug. This is goodness.

You, too, can be alert to the prompting of the Holy Spirit to benefit other people in ways that they do not deserve or expect. Now, the Lord usually directs the real extravagance toward those closest to us. There is a regular place for over-the-top goodness that is undeserved. What does that look like in your marriage, with your friends, with your colleagues, with your family, at church? A few short years ago my father lavished upon my wife and I a car we could not afford. He gave it to us because we needed it and he did not. God was working through my father to bless us beyond measure. That allowed us to give our car away to someone else. Aren't you amazed at God loving you through the wonderful people He has put in your life? We need to get the wonder of goodness flowing through your life. You don't have to invent these; just allow the Spirit of Christ to prompt you, and do not push away at the ideas because they are different, or maybe even inconvenient or require sacrifice. God's assignments to be good to others will not impoverish us; they will enrich us. Listen for God's whispers to truly benefit someone.

I cannot leave this topic of goodness without talking about one of the most forgotten relationships—you. Remember, one of the nine key relationships in your life is the one you hold with yourself. I have a hard time hearing the Lord say to me to truly benefit myself. I meet lots of people who are like me in this area. They can hear the Holy Spirit tell them to benefit others, but they have a very hard time hearing the Lord tell them to take a day to benefit themselves. "Read a book just because it would bless you." "Purchase something because you would get a lot of benefit out of it." Yesterday, I felt the prompting of the Lord to spend the time to re-read a book that had supremely benefitted me in the past (about 15 years ago). I argued back that I had already read that book and I had a lot of other things to do today. But that prompting from God would just not go away. So I took an hour this morning to get the book out and reread it as though it was my first time. What a delightful gift from the Holy Spirit! It filled my heart with hope and fired my imagination just like it had done fifteen years ago. The Spirit knows what I need to refuel and refresh; now it is up to me to listen and obey those promptings. Indeed, the Lord is good.

> "And the Lord said, "I will cause all my goodness to pass in front of you, and I will proclaim my name, the Lord, in your presence. I will have mercy on whom I will have mercy, and I will have compassion on whom I will have compassion." (Ex 33:19)

> "With this in mind, we constantly pray for you, that our God may make you worthy of his calling, and that by his power he may bring to fruition your every desire for goodness and your every deed prompted by faith." (2 Thess 1:11)

9.
Meekness Is Not Weakness

> *But the fruit of the Spirit is love, joy, peace, patience, kindness, goodness, **gentleness**, faithfulness, and self-control. (Gal 5:22,23)*

Great relationships don't just happen—they are nurtured and developed through the use of spiritual construction materials, these fruit of the Spirit we've been talking about. At the beginning of the greatest sermon ever preached, Jesus tells us, "Blessed are the meek for they shall inherit the earth"

www.ptlb.com/ grapeness-ch9

(Matt 5:5). According to Jesus Christ himself, *to be meek is the realization that the goal in life is not to be in charge, but to inhabit great relationships.*

Meekness or *gentleness,* another of the key ingredients in building great relationships, is the ability to defer to the other people in the relationship at the right time. If you expect everyone should defer to you all the time, then the relationship is really about power and control. Ask yourself whether you are flexible and adaptive to others. When you get angry with others, do you recognize that it is most likely because there is an unrealistic expectation you are projecting onto them? Do you get angry when someone argues with you or stands against your ideas? *Meekness is the antidote to anger, brooding, pouting, and whining.* It is essential in the give and take of great relationships.

The great issue with meekness is expectations. Most of our anger comes from unmet, unrealistic expectations. We have hardened our desires, wishes, and ideas into an expectation of how other people will or should respond. But they often don't act the way we want or predict. We get angry because our expectations have been trampled. We get frustrated because the other person is not doing what they should do. We get irritated because the other person is not doing what we want them to do.

To be meek, then, is to be willing to examine our expectations and adjust them to reality. Meekness is that whisper of the Holy Spirit that calls us back to sanity. When we are not meek we get swept along with a series of justifications and evidence for why what we expected to happen should have happened. I find that my selfish embrace of my expectations is what triggers and fuels my anger. If I let go of my expectations and assess the situation as it actually is, I am able to bring a whole new level of wisdom to the situation. People drive the way they drive. Some people don't return phone calls. Not everyone thinks my ideas should be followed. God whispers that I should see my anger as a sign that I am being unrealistic in my thinking. I have been unaware of how unrealistic my thinking is up to that point, but my strong reaction is the evidence that this is true. God prompts *meekness* when He wants me to readjust my response and my choices so that a positive relational result will take place.

Understand that *meekness is not weakness*. Jesus is not asking us to be weak—actually exactly the opposite. When God the Holy Spirit wants us to exercise meekness or gentleness in relationships, He will prompt us to do things that may look like accepting the other person's point of view, their way of spending time, or their choices...at least some of the time.

But, it is not weakness to:

... play a child's game with them so you can relate to them.

... listen to a teenager go on and on about the love of their life that they think will last forever and you know will be over in two weeks.

... watch a program that the family would like even though you can think of another one you would like more.

... help your child practice baseball even though you know they will never be good enough to get a scholarship to college.

... set aside your worries and concerns to look deep into your spouse's eyes and hear their pain in some small thing that happened in their day.

Look at what Ephesians 5:18-21 says,

> "And do not get drunk with wine, for that is dissipation, but be filled with the Spirit, speaking to one another in psalms and hymns and spiritual songs, singing and making melody with your heart to the Lord; always giving thanks for all things in the name of our Lord Jesus Christ to God, even the Father; and be subject to one another in the fear of Christ."

Again, one of the crucial ingredients to great relationship (not just polite relationships) is meekness or gentleness. We all must be able to defer our power, opinions, or happiness for the greater good of the relationship. We must be sensitive to the Holy Spirit as He tells us that our expectation is unrealistic in a particular case. We must learn to make thoughtful requests instead of demands. We must embrace wise adaptations instead of pouting because we did not get our way. This isn't always easy, but it is necessary many times.

When Should You Defer?

One of the problems with a culture that has 500 TV channels and hundreds of movies instantly available is that we can view exactly what we want whenever we want, and we never have to settle for something that only has a little of what we would enjoy. This kind of expectation has spilled into every relationship. Why would I do that thing with you when I would rather do this thing I like so much better? The answer is this: *You would do it when it would build a better relationship between you and the other person.*

Getting your way is not always the right thing. Look again at the construction materials required for great relationships, the fruit of the Spirit.

> *"But the fruit of the spirit is love, joy, peace, patience, kindness, goodness, gentleness, faithfulness and self-control against such things there is no law." (Gal. 5:22-23)*

These fruit must begin to show up in our lives or we will never have great relationships. And without great relationships, we will not have meaning, significance, purpose, and deep love and joy. God is alive, and He is trying to pour through you these essential ingredients of a great, successful life. When He prompts you to defer to the other person, listen. Yes, I know that you can't always defer, but there is so little meekness in our selfish day and age—any amount of deference is good. We have bad relationships, because we are too busy pushing forward what we want all the time. Our agendas and plans are more important than people. Yes, plans and agendas are important to achieve your goals but so is the forgotten secret of meekness.

Relationships are built using love, joy, peace, patience, kindness, goodness, meekness, faithfulness, and self-control. The goal of life is not for you to be rich or powerful or "happy." The goal is for you to have great relationships with God, spouse, self, friends, colleagues, Christians, family, and so on. The goal is for you to float from one great relationship to another enjoying the fruits of your labor in building these relationships.

God supplies all we need for great relationships; we just need to do the work of putting them into our lives as He prompts us. Listen for whispers to be *adaptive, flexible, and deferent*. They will be there, and it will be the voice of the Holy Spirit spurring you on.

10.
Stay the Course with Faithfulness

> *But the fruit of the Spirit is love, joy, peace, patience, kindness, goodness, gentleness, **faithfulness**, and self-control. (Gal 5:22,23)*

Faithfulness is by far one of the most interesting fruits of the Spirit. It is so unlike most of us, but it is completely and wholly like God. God's faithfulness is one of His most dominant qualities.

www.ptlb.com/
grapeness-ch10

"And he passed in front of Moses, proclaiming, "The Lord, the Lord, the compassionate and gracious God, slow to anger, abounding in love and faithfulness," (Ex 34:6)

"Your love, Lord, reaches to the heavens, your faithfulness to the skies." (Ps 36:5)

God stays faithful to hostile and undeserving people (Rom 5:8). The overarching ideas contained in the concept of faithfulness are *to stay connected, keep blessing, and provide security*. Remember that each one of the fruit of the Spirit is an aspect of love, and faithfulness is surely one of the greater aspects of love. When God prompts or whispers *stay connected to that person* or *keep blessing that person* or *keep providing security to that person,* He is saying "be faithful."

Let's take a look at each of these ideas of faithfulness in more detail.

Stay Connected

There will be people in your life that you really want to separate from, but it is clear God wants you to stay connected to them. These could be family members, friends, co-workers, neighbors, church friends, or random people in the community that you keep running into. At times, God will whisper that you need to stay connected to someone. Staying connected might look like:

... making a phone call to them.

Stay the Course with Faithfulness

... writing a note or a text.

... inviting them to coffee.

... dropping by their house.

This could be a person you are at odds with or one who has wounded you, but God is asking you to stay connected. The idea is not because any particular note or get together will change them, but your constant presence in their life will keep them attached to God and to you, and later they will come around to both.

I have talked with a number of parents who want to write off one of their children because of some offense or lifestyle that the child has pursued. And, yet, God whispers, "Faithfulness—stay connected." I just had this happen to a family I was coaching. Their adult son got involved in drugs, and their desire was to distance themselves from him. But the father sensed that God was saying *stay connected; be faithful*. Because of this whisper, the father was able to work with the son and begin solving the drug and relationship problem with his son. Staying connected is not easy and it is not immediate, but it is what God whispers to us about some of the people in our life.

Let me be clear that God does not whisper "faithfulness" in regards to all of the people who are currently in our lives. There are some people who you need to get distance from—people that you need to cut out of your life that may be harming you or influencing you to participate in evil or manipulating you in some way. If this is the case, you need physical, emotional, or mental distance from them. Some people have a rescue mindset, which causes them to want to stay connected to and help everyone. You may not be the answer for that person, even though you desperately want to see them get help. Let God do the whispering.

Keep Blessing

Another aspect of faithfulness is one of blessing. God does not just keep hammering us with messages of what we should do or what we should stop doing. He blesses us and gives us little delights, even while we may be ignoring Him in certain areas of our lives. There will be times when God whispers to you that you are to bless someone who He wants you to stay connected to. Sometimes it is the person that you least feel like blessing at the time. Other times it is a somewhat distant person. We need to realize that we are God's delivery agents. There are many times when He blesses us so that we can bless others.

As His agents, God will often have us bless those closest to us. I can remember a number of times as a pastor when members of my church would call me and say, "I received an unexpected bonus at work and I know it is not for me; do we have anyone in the church who has a need?" It was always amazing how it worked out, because God would prompt me to say, "Yes, we have someone who can't pay their mortgage this month, and your amount matches their need!"

I have watched family members bless the prodigal for years with little gifts here or there. Eventually, the wayward person wakes up and embraces God and the love of their family. Faithfulness to friends, family, and neighbors is not normal these days, and doing so sticks out like a sore thumb. Listen to God's promptings. Is God asking you to bless someone in your life who really doesn't deserve to be blessed, but He wants you to get a gift card for them, or buy them a cup of coffee? Don't ignore these promptings.

Provide Security

Faithfulness is also manifested by providing security to someone. This may be physical, emotional, or mental security. There are times when God will urge us to stay faithful to a friend or family member who is on the ragged edge of life. Often when a person is running from God or something else in their life, they are at the edges of safety or health. We may provide a place to stay or a regular meal or a bus pass or some new clothes or a regular counseling visit or job training. I can remember taking a young man into my house when his parents kicked him out. I was able to help him get started in a work program and finish high school. For a brief few months, I provided security for him to get his life together after the expulsion from his home. This person you are helping may not want to turn around or stop being irritating, but they do need the security that you can provide.

When God prompts you to help provide security for another person, this often moves into more of a long-term commitment. One of the ways to make sure that you are really helping the person is to work with all the wonderful charitable organizations that are ready to help people in the particular situation that your friend or family member is in. These organizations have seen it all and can help you stay balanced, as you want to help. I have seen a number of people actually harm a person's recovery by offering too much help too soon. Our family has volunteered with groups that help those who have been trafficked for sex, those who rescue animals from abuse, and those who help the homeless. Each of these experiences has been rewarding and truly helpful. Our family also sponsors children in other parts of the world so that they can go to school and have a warm meal. This is exercising faithfulness by providing security.

God wants us to grow gardens of relational fruit and enjoy the wonders of the relationships that gather around the fruit we grow. Life is relationships. When you listen to the Lord prompt you to engage with people through faithfulness, you grow a rich, relational life. Listen for His voice that says, "stay connected," "keep blessing," or "provide security." He will guide you in growing the fruit of faithfulness, and everyone will be blessed.

11.
Moderate Your Desires with Self-Control

> *But the fruit of the Spirit is love, joy, peace, patience, kindness, goodness, gentleness, faithfulness, and **self-control**.* (Gal 5:22,23)

People have many different desires that flare up over the course of their lives—desires to work more hours, to have more fun, to buy more things, to do what they want. But if we are to grow a truly healthy set of relationships, and thus a successful life, our desires at various times must be moderated,

www.ptlb.com/
grapeness-ch11

or else these very good desires can damage or kill a relationship if they are let loose or left unchecked. This is why the Holy Spirit wants us to learn how to exercise self-control.

For many people, *self-control* only has to do with weight management and sexual desire, but the Holy Spirit has so much more in mind when He included self-control in the basic fruits of the Spirit. The idea of self-control is to *moderate your desires for the good of the relationship.*

Years ago, I really wanted to pastor a larger church in another part of the country. This church alluded to the fact that I would be selected for the job. I had preached there on a few occasions and had been very well received. When I began praying and discussing this opportunity and my deep desire to do this with Dana, my wife, she jokingly said, "I hope you can come back and visit us on the weekends, because we are staying here. I really want you to get what you want, but that move at this time in our family's life would be way too disruptive, and I don't think it is wise." I remember in my prayer time the Lord showed me that He agreed with her. God was asking me to moderate my desire for the sake of my girls and our relationship as a family. I also asked a number of mentors, even the ones who wanted to see me take the "promotion," and they all agreed that the family was more important. God was whispering *self-control.*

I do not regret doing what God asked me to do. I would make the same choice now that I did then, but I would just make the decision more quickly. The relationship I have with my children, and the emotional, mental, and spiritual health that each of them has because of the roots they have put down is priceless. Our marriage and family relationships are more robust because I partnered with God (and my wife) to moderate my desire.

The mother of one family I worked with desired a more fun-filled life than she currently had. Raising two daughters and cooking dinners every night was not her idea of the good life. She was bored and restless. As a very attractive woman, she attracted a lot of male attention, especially when she went out with her girlfriends. Eventually, she had a choice to make. She could choose to moderate her desire for "good times" or throw caution to the wind and let her real desires out. I talked with her before she had made her final decision, pleading with her to practice self-control. I warned her, "If you do this, you will have a lot of 'fun,' but you will also collect diseases, beatings, scars, and most importantly, you will break the heart of these two little girls that adore you." She chose not to moderate her desires and pursued the wild party scene with various men. She traveled the world from party to party, but five years after she left, she came back—older, bent by the booze, broke, diseased, and wounded by numerous men. The most tragic part was that her daughters wanted no part of a relationship with the mother who had abandoned them. This is why the Spirit whispers *self control*, as He knows that to do otherwise will make a mess out of the situation.

Strong Desires

Let's talk a little about our desires. The dictionary defines a desire as a "strong feeling of wanting to do or have something or wishing for something to happen." This list of desires can be either helpful or destructive depending upon the relationship and the level to which this desire is allowed to dominate or overpower what is beneficial:

power	control
rest	food
drink	pleasure
money	sexual expression
comfort	security
ambition	authority
knowledge	possessions
change	involvement

It's easy to see how any of these can destroy a relationship if it overshadows all other needs and desires in a relationship. And yet many times, the screams within us of a particular desire is so strong that we just keep pushing to have it at a rate or level that is not helpful to the relationship. Consider the fable of King Midas. He was so greedy for gold that he wished everything he touched would be turned to gold. In the fictional story he was granted his wish and he thought it was wonderful; that is, until he touched his daughter and she turned to gold. He thought he wanted everything to be gold until the desire destroyed one of the most precious relationships he had. All desires have to be moderated at times. This is why we need self-control.

It is our world, our culture, which tries to trick us into making our desires our "gods." We are told that we need to do what makes us happy. We are told that we should be happy all the time. We are presented a dizzying array of choices and then asked to decide which one we want—fast. Our desires are a part of us and many are helpful in propelling us forward. But if any of them are dialed up to one hundred, they can be destructive. If our desires become our "gods," everyone will lose, including us. The way to really attain success and a great life is to enjoy the things of this life within the context of loving God, loving our spouse, our family, our colleagues, our friends, and ourselves (1 Tim 4:4,5).

When to Moderate Your Desires

In every relationship, there will be times when you have to moderate a desire for a period of time for the sake of that relationship. Most work places require that you moderate your desire for breaks and fun during the 8+ hours you are at the work place. In fact they fire people who don't moderate that desire. Sometimes you will have to moderate your desire to say things that you think are true, because it is clear that the people in the relationship are not prepared to hear what you have to say. Saying those things would only cause them to hate you and push you away from having any influence now or in the future.

While I was raising my girls, I had to listen to the Spirit prompting me to moderate my desire to over-protect them, to tell them every right answer, to keep them from making some mistakes. I wanted my girls to be completely protected, and it was very hard to realize that my desire for their complete protection had to change as they grew up. They needed to make choices on their own and I had to learn to be okay with it. It took a great deal of self-control.

When you view self-control through the lenses of the nine relationships in your life, try to figure out what desires come up within you that may need to be controlled for the good of that relationship. You may have "good" relationships with your kids, but the goal is to build great relationships with them. That requires you to be in tune with what is needed for this higher level of relating with those in your life.

A few questions to ask might be:

- What desires do I have that need to be controlled to make my relationship with God great?

- What areas of self-control do I need to exercise to make a great relationship with my self?

- What desires do I need to control in the area of my marriage in order to make it great?

And so on...

God the Holy Spirit wants to whisper to you about which desires need to be moderated and when. As you are interacting in society or at work or with your family, you need to be alert to the whispers of God to moderate a strong desire. Sometimes you have to keep your mouth shut when you want to talk. Sometimes you need to be generous with your money when you want to hold on to it. Sometimes you need to hold back on your ambition when you want to scream, "I want to do that!" Sometimes you have to not purchase the thing you want because that money needs to be invested or used to do something more important for another person.

Take the time to be reflective in each of your relationships. Ask God to prompt you about which desire in each relationship needs to be moderated to build the healthiest relationship. It will be different for each one. Let God know that you are listening and find ways to partner with Him in moderating those desires for the sake of the relationship.

Remember, you are not backing off from accomplishing what God wants you to accomplish. You are instead pushing forward with what God truly wants and what you want: tremendous, righteous relationships.

12.
Practice Standing in Each Garden

To grow a spirit-led life of success, you must adapt to your role as a relational gardener, who Jesus wants to partner with to have a delightful life full of true success. Listen for the whispers of His Spirit to add some more love, joy, peace, patience, and so forth, into a particular relationship.

I have developed a number of spiritual exercises that can help focus your listening to the Holy Spirit in the midst of your busy day. Some of them will work wonderfully for you,

www.ptlb.com/
grapeness-ch12

and some of them will just not be as helpful. Try each of the exercises and stay with the ones that allow you to hear the promptings and whispers of the Holy Spirit to produce His fruit.

Begin by practicing to mentally stand in each of your gardens (Marriage/Dating, Family, Work, Finances, God, Friends, Church, Community, Self) and ask God about each fruit of the Spirit. You are looking for what God wants to do through you on that day in that relationship. You ultimately want to partner with God, so if God wants to display patience through you, then get ready to display patience. Go through all nine fruit of the Spirit in each relationship and let God speak.

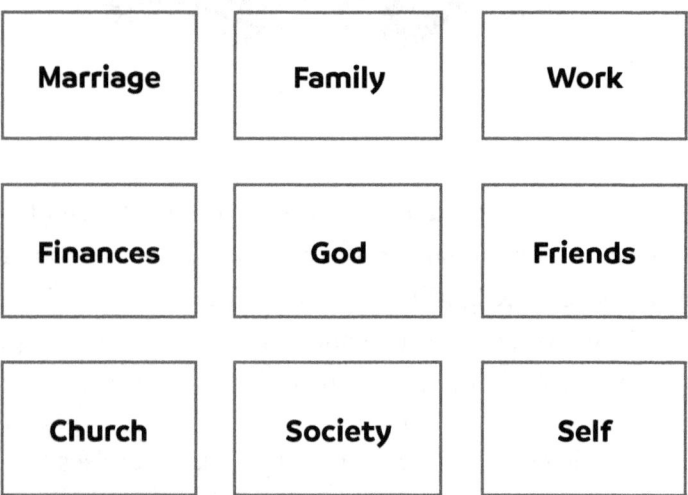

For this to work, I have found that it is important to be mentally standing in the relationship as you ask the question. Sometimes I find it is harder to hear the Lord clearly when the person(s) I'm asking about is nearby. Sometimes I am more alive to the whispers of the Holy Spirit when I am presently engaged in the actual relationship. The give and take of reality helps me to be aware of the Holy Spirit's prompting for me to partner with Him—to do something different than I would normally do.

Begin asking God to guide you more directly than you may have ever asked before. God is alive and He will guide you. He wants to partner with you to build a dynamic life. Most people have been going all cowboy (rebelling, doing it on their own) and not listening, not asking, not doing what He prompts when He prompts it. You and I have access to the most wise and powerful being in the whole universe—*we should take more advantage of Him!*

It's All about the Pause

The key to this exercise is to ask God and listen for the response. We know that God is alive and wants to communicate with those who are believers (John 1:12; Rom 8:14). If we are going to have the most fulfilling, most successful Christian life, then we must be able to *hear the whispers* of the Spirit of God. We know what He is going to say. He is going to tell us to increase the amount of love, joy, peace, patience, kindness, goodness, faithfulness, and self-control in our lives so that our relationships can flourish. It is this interactive relationship between you and God that is important.

Let's walk through this together.

"Lord, do you want me to **love** more in this relationship?" (Pause. Let Him speak to you about meeting specific needs, pursuing someone's soul, or pleasing them.) I have found that God will often prompt, suggest, or give me a picture of a particular activity (vacuuming, lifting a heavy load, opening a door, etc.). I need to let God's prompting flow through me into action.

"Lord, do you want me to add more **joy** here in this relationship?" (Pause. Let Him speak to you about not being cynical, looking for the good, being encouraging, and so forth.) How does God want joy to flow through you in this particular relationship?

"Lord, do you want more **peace** here?" (Pause. Let Him speak to you about this relationship and harmony, order, and calm.) When we ask questions like this, we are tying into the ultimate source of power, knowledge, wisdom, and love. He knows what is needed for this relationship. When He brings something to your mind that lines up with peace in the relationship—harmony, order, or calm—then do it.

"Lord, do you want me to add more **patience** in this relationship?" (Pause. Let Him speak to you about giving the other person or yourself more time, room for growth, or opportunities.) I have found that God is willing to wait years, even decades, to see a person develop (look at Abraham, Moses, and Paul). There are times when God prompts me to postpone a conversation I really want to have with someone (my wife, kids, colleagues, friends, or others), because they cannot handle what I want to say at that time. There are some conversations I waited fifteen years to have with my children. Your impatience and my impatience is not God's, and He wants the conversation to be at the right time for the benefit of the other person and the relationship.

"Lord, do you want me to add more **kindness** to this relationship?" (Pause. Let Him speak to you about how you should be helping the other person.) Kindness is pleasant helpfulness. Sometimes we try to help people, but they pick up resentment or distractedness in the help we try to give. That is not what we're after. We want our help to be a pleasant experience for them and us.

"Lord, do you want me to add more **goodness** to this relationship?" (Pause. Let Him speak to you about truly benefitting the other person in some way.) When God is good to us, it means mercy, grace, physical benefit, spiritual blessings, emotionally supportive, and so forth. Sometimes when God wants to get my attention in this area of goodness, He will whisper, "Forgive them;" "Give them more than they deserve;" "Bless them with a specific encouragement;" "Give them some money;" "Help them do that task."

"Lord, do you want me to add more **meekness** to this relationship?" (Pause. Let Him speak to you about managing your anger, irritation, and frustration.) God wants us to be much more adaptive than we want to be most of the time.

When He whispers *meekness* or *gentleness,* He wants us to realize where we have unrealistic expectations of that other person or the relationship. He is whispering that He wants us to make wise adaptations. He is prompting us to make thoughtful requests to get the relationship back on track.

"Lord, do you want me to add more **faithfulness** to this relationship?" (Pause. Let Him speak to you about staying connected to a person or a relationship longer than you may want to.) God will often prompt us about a person or a relationship that we have put on the back burner. This is often about faithfulness. He wants us to contact that person or stay connected to that person in some way. Relationships can die and some should, but God will also prompt you to keep a relationship alive that would die without some effort and energy on your part. Partner with God and let Him guide you to keep connected to relationships that will be important for you or for the other person in the future.

"Lord, do you want me to add more **self-control** to this relationship?" (Pause. Let Him speak to you about where you need to moderate your desires to enhance this relationship.) All of us have various desires in each of our relationships; many of them are helpful, but a number of them are destructive in the levels that we want to pursue them. I can think of the times that I desperately wanted my wife to enjoy my favorite hobbies at the level I enjoyed them. I have watched people emotionally vomit all the pain and sorrow in their life onto their new friend and drive them away. I have watched men and women let their ambition come out unchecked, which destroyed their marriage, family, and friendships. God wants to have us moderate our desires so that the relationships will be the healthiest. He may want to talk with you about one of your passions that could be destroying parts of your relational life.

After you have done this exercise a few dozen times, you may just be able to mentally stand in the relationship and think through the fruit of the Spirit very quickly and have God and you zero in on what He wants you to do for that relationship for maximum relational health. It's a process worth pursuing—a way to develop this amazing relationship with the Almighty God.

Conclusion: A Look at Proverbs 11:30

"The fruit of the righteous is a tree of life and he who is wise wins souls." (Prov 11:30)

Through the observations of Solomon a thousand years before Christ, God tells us in a slightly different way that strong, living, healthy relationships are the purpose of life. These types of relationships are the wonderful results of a well-lived life. They are the fruit of the righteous, deep, and life-giving relationships. The apostle Paul tells us in Galatians 5:22-23 that God the Holy Spirit wants to pour through us the spiritual essentials that create great relationships: the fruit of the Spirit.

www.ptlb.com/
grapeness-conclusion

When a person stays within the boundaries of the Ten Commandments and feeds their nine relationship gardens with love, joy, peace, patience, kindness, goodness, meekness, faithfulness, and self-control, they can thrive from the relationships that develop. It is the use of these specific aspects of love that builds a great life. A recent study on loneliness in older people suggested that being lonely cuts eight years off of life. But having lots of people you care about and who care about you prolongs and enriches your life.

Let's take a deeper look at the Hebrew words and thoughts in this insightful verse through the observations I made in my books *Breakfast with Solomon* and *A Devotional Commentary on Proverbs*.

> *"The fruit of the righteous is a tree of life and he who is wise wins souls." (Prov 11:30)*

This verse means the results of righteous living are sustaining and life giving. Also in the Hebrew understanding of the biblical era, fruit was the sweetest thing one could have other than honey. To be enjoying fruit meant that one was having dessert. One was rewarded for their perseverance, work, and patience with fruit. When one lives within the boundaries of righteousness and blesses others through positive righteousness, they begin a continual feasting on the sweetness of life.

tree of life

The Hebrew understanding of the tree of life was that which

prolonged life, sustained it, and gave it a quality of existence that was beyond mere biological existence. In this case, the fruit of the righteous life is not just a dessert or extra element, but what sustains life and allows it to be life beyond just biology.

Solomon is saying that the positive way of living (that is righteousness) produces a kind and quality of life. Do you want to have a higher quality of life? Then give up on the selfish route and instead find ways to be a positive benefit into the lives of those around you, so that they expect good and not evil from you. Remember *life is relationships.* No matter how much you possess, if you do not have close people to share it with, then your victories are hollow. Life is lived at a higher plain, with soul-to-soul contact and connection.

wise

This is the person who applies knowledge in a way that is mutually beneficial to others, yourself, and glorifying to God. The wise person is not after their own selfish ends but the good of the family, the good of the society, the good of the business, and the glory of God.

wins

This is the Hebrew word laqach, which means to take, to accept, to capture, to seize, to win. Solomon gives us a clue that we should focus on the person's soul; not their body or material possessions. The person who focuses on connecting and influencing the soul (the wise person) has a much easier time in life.

souls

This is the Hebrew word *nephesh,* which means *soul, living being.* It is what happened when God breathed into Adam and he became a living soul. The soul is the inner part of the person. The real you is the collection of your experiences, education, skills, and so forth. Your soul is the software that is running the hardware called your body. The fool tries to win bodies, through power, authority, seduction, deception, and the like. But the wise person tries to capture the soul of the person for the project, the relationship.

Jesus gave us the secret to success in Matthew 22:37-39. Another way to say it is, "My purpose in life is to love God with all my heart, soul, mind, and strength, and my neighbor as myself." Everything of value will come out of the relationships I build fulfilling those verses. All of the money I make; all of the fun I have; all of the significance I experience; all of the change I contribute to the world; all of the legacy I leave—all of it will come out of the relationships I develop. Our culture tries to convince us that meaning, significance, power, and joy come from tasks and ideas and accomplishments and things, but without relationships, we don't get to do the tasks and bring the ideas to fruition!

Solomon calls *the way of the righteous a tree of life.* When we have deep and interactive relationships, it brings new purpose, meaning, and significance to our lives.

About Gil Stieglitz

Dr. Gil Stieglitz is an author, speaker, catalyst, professor, and leadership consultant. He speaks to thousands of people every year about building healthy and successful relationships. Gil currently serves as Discipleship Pastor at Bayside Church, a dynamic multi-site church on the north side of Sacramento, CA. He served for five years as Executive Pastor of Adventure Christian Church in Roseville, CA. He is an adjunct professor at Western Seminary (Sacramento Campus), a church consultant for Thriving Churches International, and Founder and President of Principles To Live By, a discipleship and publishing non-profit. He has served on the board of a number of non-profit groups to help start churches, revitalize pastors, and rescue minors. He has been a denominational executive for thirteen years with the Evangelical Church of America and was the senior pastor at a mid-sized church in Southern California for seventeen years. Gil has a heart for helping people become all that God wants them to be. His believes that "Great Life Is Great Relationships."

To learn more about Gil, his books, resources, and speaking and consulting opportunities, visit **www.ptlb.com.**

More from Principles To Live By

Books

Becoming a Godly Husband
Becoming Courageous
Breakfast with Solomon, Volumes 1 - 3
Breaking Satanic Bondage
Deep Happiness: the Eight Secrets
Delighting in God
Delighting in Jesus
Developing a Christian Worldview
God's Radical Plan for Wives
Going Deep In Prayer: Forty Days of In-Depth Prayer
Keeping Visitors
Leading a Thriving Ministry
Marital Intelligence
Mission Possible: Winning the Battle over Temptation
Proverbs: a Devotional Commentary, Volumes 1 - 2
Satan and the Origin of Evil
Secrets of God's Armor
Spiritual Disciplines of a C.H.R.I.S.T.I.A.N.

The Schemes of Satan
They Laughed When I Wrote Another Book about Prayer, Then They Read It
Touching the Face of God: Forty Days of Adoring God
Weapons of Righteousness Study Guides
Why There Has to Be a Hell

Online Video Courses

Mission Possible: Winning the Battle over Temptation
Becoming a Godly Husband

Audio Files

Becoming a Godly Parent
Biblical Meditation: the Keys of Transformation
Deep Happiness: the Eight Secrets
Everyday Spiritual Warfare Series
God's Guide to Handling Money
Marital Intelligence: There are Only Five Problems in Marriage
Intensive Spiritual Warfare Series
Spiritual War Surrounding Money
The Four Keys to a Great Family
The Ten Commandments
Raising Your Leadership Level: Double Your Impact
Spiritual Warfare: Using the Weapons of God to Win Spiritual Battles
Weapons of Righteousness Series